BRIGHT IDEAS

Supply Teaching

D1395841

Written by Alison Vickers

Published by Scholastic Publications Ltd,
Villiers House, Clarendon Avenue,
Leamington Spa, Warwickshire CV32 5PR

© 1993 Scholastic Publications Ltd

Written by Alison Vickers
Edited by Felicity Kendall and Jo Saxelby
Illustrated by Lesley Smith
Designed by Micky Pledge
Cover design by Keith Martin
Cover photograph by Martyn Chillmaid
Artwork by Castle Graphics, Kenilworth
Printed in Great Britain by Loxley
Brothers Ltd, Sheffield

British Library
Cataloguing-in-Publication Data
A catalogue record for this book is available from the
British Library.

ISBN 0-590-53044-5

All rights reserved. This book is sold subject to the
condition that it shall not, by way of trade or otherwise,
be lent, hired out or otherwise circulated without the
publisher's prior consent in any form of binding or
cover other than that in which it is published and
without a similar condition, including this condition,
being imposed upon the subsequent purchaser.

No part of this publication may be reproduced, stored
in a retrieval system, or transmitted, in any form or by
any means, electronic, mechanical, photocopying,
recording or otherwise, without the prior permission of
the publisher, except where photocopying for
educational purposes within a school or other
educational establishment is expressly permitted in the
text.

Acknowledgement
The author would like to thank the staff and
children of all the schools where she has
tried out these ideas, colleagues for their
suggestions and family and friends for their
support.

Contents

Part 1 – preparation

This book is specifically for supply teachers or any teacher who finds him or herself having to take over a class at a minute's notice. It also gives general advice to anyone contemplating supply teaching.

There are many advantages to supply teaching. It is highly stimulating to move from one school and class to another. You are constantly being refreshed with new ideas for work with the children and for classroom management. It can give you an insight into how various schools operate before you commit yourself to a permanent job. It saves a lot of time, for although you have the usual preparation and marking to do, you do not have to concern yourself with displays, staff meetings, parents meetings, out-of-school activities and writing reports. You can also repeat more successful lessons with other classes or in other schools, thus saving on preparation time. It is a very flexible job too so you can control your working life more easily to fit in with other commitments.

GETTING STARTED

If you have just retired or have decided you would like a change from contract teaching, you just need to tell your local education authority about your wish to supply teach. However, if you have been out of teaching for more than three years you will need to fill in a form from your local authority. If you have moved authorities since you last taught, you will need to approach the local Education Office and your references will be taken up. This may take a little while as your documents from your previous authority will have to be moved across, so be prepared to wait a few weeks. Your name will then go on a central list and be circulated to headteachers in your area.

Many headteachers do not need to refer to the central supply list as they have their own contacts, but they are often very glad to take on someone who lives locally as he or she can come into school at very short notice. Consider how far you are prepared to travel, bearing in mind the extra time you will need to get organised and to rearrange your day if you are called in at short notice. Then find out the names and addresses of primary schools within your travelling range and either ring them up, or find out the headteachers' names and write directly to them. The letter should contain a very brief synopsis of your career and could indicate your preferred age group (if this concerns you). Make yourself familiar with the location of these schools so that you know the most suitable routes to drive there and the availability of car parking, or the best way to get there using public transport.

Once you have decided to commit yourself to doing supply teaching, then it is as well to prepare yourself in advance. Do not expect all classrooms to be fully equipped or expect to be able to find all essential items, and the children may not be able to help you.

If you have been out of teaching for a number of years check whether your local authority runs courses for supply or returning teachers or volunteer to help out with some activities at your local school. This will help to build up your confidence. You could borrow National Curriculum documents, familiarise yourself with the computers and check on anything else that might be of concern to you.

Your basic kit

You will need the following items:
- a diary with your teacher's number in it (some authorities will also require your National Insurance number and a payroll number);
- a service record card (if you are given one);
- red, black and blue biros;
- a good eraser, ruler, a few sharp pencils and a pencil sharpener;
- black and yellow fine felt-tipped pens and a thick black felt-tipped marker pen;
- whistle, trainers or plimsols;
- dictionary, stand-by story-book or anthology;
- Blu-Tack, drawing pins;
- glue stick, adhesive tape;
- large pair of good quality scissors;
- correction pen (we all make mistakes in the register at some time!).

Other useful, but non-essential, items include:
- tracksuit (for games or if someone throws paint over you!);
- coloured chalks, board protractor (available from school suppliers – see 'Useful addresses' page 128);
- paper fasteners, paper clips, stapler;
- self-adhesive notelets, e.g. 'Post-its';

- wallpaper paste;
- small bottle of washable PVA medium;
- a few glue spreaders;
- string, hat-elastic, a few darning needles;
- tape measure;
- some sheets of plain A4 paper;
- gold stars or incentive stickers or stamps;
- map of the world (ideally Peters' Projection, as available from Christian Aid – see 'Useful addresses' page 128).

Ideas folders
The next stage is to plan some ideas for the various age groups you hope to cover. If you have material left over from previous teaching it makes sense to use this. The easiest way to organise these ideas is to put all the items for one theme, for a particular age group, in a transparent zip folder. The folder might contain photocopiable sheets, examples of the things you want the children to do, a poster, workcards, a story-book and, of course, a list of the things that you hope to cover on the theme. On the outside of the folder you could write a list of the extra things you will need to take from your own, or a school, resources collection (see 'Useful things to collect' below).

You could also make 'emergency' folders for each age group. These would contain items which would keep the children occupied when they have finished their set work. These could include: maths (sum) cards, photocopiable pages, additional workcards, tracing cards, handwriting pattern cards and puzzle pages.

One word of warning, do not rely on photocopiable pages as your sole teaching aid. Virtually all primary schools have photocopiers but these machines have been known to break down, so have some other ideas or materials ready.

Finally, keep a 'running list' of what you intend to teach, divided into schools and classes, in a very accessible place.

Useful things to collect
The items listed below are useful resources for the classroom and worth collecting:
- old travel catalogues (particularly world-wide ones);
- old gift, household, clothes and plant catalogues;
- a few magazines;
- old Christmas and birthday cards and postcards;
- buttons, shells and feathers;
- cardboard tubes and old egg boxes.

It is also worthwhile finding out whether you have a 'scrapbox' facility locally where you can purchase excess factory materials very cheaply, for example card, coloured, shiny, crêpe or tissue paper and off-cuts of felt and leather.

If you have the storage space, it is also a good idea to have a large roll of white paper (check your local printer for off-cuts). Alternatively, you might purchase a large flipchart pad. This means you can write your instructions and draw diagrams or illustrations for the class in advance; this, of course, will save you time in the classroom and is reusable.

Useful things to make and buy
If you intend to continue supply teaching for some time it is worthwhile making or buying the following items (you can sometimes pick up useful educational games and books from jumble or car boot sales):
- a simple picture lotto game;
- dominoes;
- dice (large, small and plain);
- tracing cards (you could cut up some unused children's colouring books and stick the pictures on to cards);
- handwriting pattern cards (draw some simple, large writing patterns on strips of card about 12×4cm);
- ten thick A4–A5 size cards, each with a number from 1 to 10 (these are for sorting and counting objects in the Reception class);
- small cards with individual letters on them (to make words);
- small cards with simple, common words written on them (to make sentences);
- a thick, covered card with numbers 1 to 10 written on in large clear figures;
- puzzle cards (cut up some old puzzle books and mount the pages on card, or use pages from such books as the *Teacher Timesaver* series (1992–, Scholastic);
- maths (sum) cards (these are regarded as rather 'old-fashioned' in most schools, but children enjoy the novelty value; they are good for re-enforcing basic number work, when children are working individually at their own level and they are useful 'fill-ins' at the end of a lesson);
- photocopiable sheets on basic English, maths and science work (either make your own or purchase one or two books).

Teachers' centres
Find out whether your local teachers' centre will lend you books and resources.

Your 'early morning call'

When you receive your request to come in for the day, assuming that you know how to find the school, you'll need to know the following essential information.

- When do they start and finish? Do not assume all schools start at nine o'clock!
- What age are the children? Most schools operate by calling children by their National Curriculum year group, but not all do.

IN SCHOOL

First, locate the headteacher and find out the following:

- break and lunch times;
- assembly time and procedure;
- procedure, if any, for collecting the children from the playground;
- registration procedure (if a dinner register is necessary and if all registers have to be returned to the office);
- PE and swimming lesson times and procedures for the children to change their clothes;
- television times and procedures;
- if you are on playground duty, and the procedures;
- children with specific problems in your class (some teachers prefer to make their own judgements on children, but you may find such information helpful);
- any ancillary help.

Some schools have a booklet for supply teachers with this kind of information in, which is very useful.

Organising your day

When you have established the timetable you will quickly need to plan how you are going to organise the class activities for the day. You may be constrained by a specific timetable and expected to teach certain subjects at allocated times, or may find yourself team teaching and be asked to teach specific subjects to different groups of children. If the children are used to a very formal education it would probably be wise to carry on the tradition and have the class all doing something similar on your first visit. However, if the class appears to be used to an integrated day and the classroom is set up for this, have a variety of activities going on at once.

The children's work

It is usually better to avoid letting the children work in their class books for the following reasons:

- you will not be aware of the way the class teacher likes work to be presented and marked;
- you will be unfamiliar with the children's standard of work and, therefore, something which might be acceptable to you may not be for the class teacher (and vice versa).

Avoid letting the children use poor quality paper, unless for rough drafts. They must feel that the work they do with you is to be valued and they won't if asked to work on scruffy paper. If this is the only paper you are offered, you will have to decide whether to offer your own paper at your own expense.

Ideas for presentation

One idea that works well is to help the children to make their own individual books; this has the advantage of keeping all the work for the day together. Most of the photocopiable pages in this book are A4 landscape and have been designed so that they can be folded in half satisfactorily to form the two centre pages of a book. One or two more A4 pages can be added and then stapled together. Alternatively, you could make a folded frieze-style book, or if the children are going to be working on different-sized or shaped paper, then their work could be stuck on to sugar paper which could be cut up and made into individual books.

Another idea is to make class books where all the work on one aspect of the theme is fastened together, for example a 'shape book' or a 'space book'. Some teachers put these books in the book corner and it is very rewarding when you come back at a later stage to see children reading these in their leisure time. Some themes lend themselves to a large class book (such as a class newspaper).

Acceptable standards

Follow the class teacher's rules about using pens, pencils, erasers, correction pens or fluid and guide lines. Sometimes it is hard to gauge on a first visit whether some children are being lazy and 'trying it on' because you are a supply teacher, or whether they are slow and genuinely trying hard. If you are unsure, ask to see some class books of that child's work. A quick look around the walls will give you a rough idea of what the class teacher accepts. Make some encouraging remarks about this and state that this is what you expect too.

Marking

The way teachers mark is very much an individual preference, particularly for creative writing. Some correct every spelling and punctuation in sight, while others will correct a few errors and concentrate on constructive general comments. If you are anxious to follow the teacher's pattern, you need only to check in the children's books. It is preferable, if possible, to mark the work with the children present or at lunch time; in this way you can catch any 'lazy' children or those who have misunderstood before the end of the day.

Hearing children read

Most teachers (and children) will appreciate it if you find time to hear some of the children read. There are three main approaches operating in primary schools at present: the traditional reading scheme; a colour-coded system, where children choose books marked with a particular colour; and the real books approach, where the children have a free choice. If the children are reading from 'real books', you may be expected to read to the child or the child will try and join in with a few words, depending on the level of the book. For a detailed explanation of this system see Liz Waterland's book *Read With Me* (1985, Thimble Press).

Discipline

Some teachers have a naturally authoritative presence and discipline is rarely a problem. If you do not have this personality, it may be wise to plan in your mind what you will do if certain situations arise. Where possible, it is best to have a positive approach and comment on good behaviour and work. Some class teachers operate table points and, if so, it is recommended that you carry on with these.

Younger children respond very well to stars, which could be stuck on their work or taped on to their clothes, for helpful or good behaviour; alternatively, you could use incentive stamps or stickers. Try and avoid confrontation and threats if possible, but when behaviour is unacceptable you will have to decide on your own set of sanctions, whether this is to keep children in at playtimes or exempt them from some activity.

Perhaps the hardest part of the supply teacher's job is coping with 'problem' children. Most children are happy to have a change of face and activities, but a few highly disturbed children cannot cope with change and may cause problems. If the behaviour becomes disruptive to the other children and your teaching, you will have to have the child removed for a while to calm down.

Other problems can arise from those who have just started school and those who are soon going to leave. Some Reception children can be very upset by a new face. You could try calming them down by sitting them on your lap and reading a story to the class or doing finger rhymes, then set the children off on relaxed, familiar activities involving some play. Some children at the top end of the school can get a little cheeky — they know you are only there for a day and will play up. You will need to be firm and, if necessary, split up the troublemakers.

All children respond well to good humour and hopefully, if your activities are interesting and novel, the children will soon become engrossed with them. If, however, at the end of the day you feel very unhappy with your relationship with a class, it is better to be honest with the headteacher about this for your sake and the children's.

Records

If you have time, class teachers are grateful if you can leave a note about the activities you covered during the day. You could also include a list of children you heard read and any relevant comments about certain children.

You may find the simplest way of keeping track of what you have taught is to write in your diary the school, class and theme covered on that day. Then transfer this to a file which is divided into schools and classes, so you have a record of what you have covered with each class. Then up-date your 'running record' and write a new theme alongside the class you have just taught.

THE YEAR GROUPS

The themes in this book are presented in year groups. Since you may be asked to take a group with which you are not familiar, some average expectations and generalised classroom set-ups are given below.

Reception

You may well find that you have some ancillary help for part of your day if you are teaching a Reception class, and it would be a good idea to plan your more ambitious activities for when you have additional help available. If you find yourself with a large Reception class and no help, you will have to organise your day so that you only have one or two new activities going on at a time, and have a number of familiar activities for the children which do not need much help. Children of this age cannot concentrate for very long, so keep your explanations as brief and clear as possible. Also, if you have a long period (over an hour) without a break, try and divide the time into class lessons and individual or group activities of about 20 minutes each. Reception class children love finger rhymes and action songs (it doesn't matter if you can't sing!) and there is no rule to say that a story has to be at the end of the day. The children may be used to wandering from one activity to another or you may prefer to have a 'changing over' time, so encouraging the children to stay with one activity for ten minutes or so.

The majority of chidren in the Reception class will be working towards Level 1 of the National Curriculum. They will expect you to write simple sentences for them to copy. However, some children may find this difficult and may wish just to go over the top of your writing. This is easier if you write in yellow felt-tipped pen.

Monica Meridith   Age 5

You may find the children are using 'emergent writing'. Initially, the children are encouraged to make their own marks and 'scribbles', which are their writing and then read back what they have written. They are also introduced to conventional letters and words and then encouraged to use a mixture of known and made-up words. Finally, they transfer to totally conventional writing. 'Sentence makers' is another popular system in use in many primary schools. Each child has a folder containing a variety of printed words, arranged grammatically, and a collection of other words written by the teacher. The children place these words in a plastic rod to make sentences which they then copy.

In mathematics the children will be experimenting with a variety of apparatus and doing simple sorting, matching, counting and number recognition activities. Most will still be working with numbers up to ten.

Generally, it is best to have the tables prepared for the children with all the materials that they need. Avoid painting, unless you have a small class, extra help or a very mature class. Some may need help with cutting and gluing activities. If possible, avoid letting them have a free choice. It is preferable, if you can, to get out the activities in advance (then you will know how and where they go back) and let them choose from these.

Allow at least 15 minutes changing time after PE if you have a large class (many will need help with buttons and shoe laces).

Years 1 and 2

Children in this age group (sometimes called middle and top infants) will have been in school at least a year and so will be familiar with school routine. You may find there is a great range of ability in the class: some may only be able to read a few words and will need to have words written for them to copy, whereas others will be fluent readers and writing competently by themselves. They will have a greater concentration span than Reception children and should be able to listen attentively or work for up to 30 minutes on one activity.

Those writing independently will still need considerable help with spelling and may bring you word cards or word books. Hopefully, the classroom will have picture word books or charts or words round the room to which the children should be encouraged to refer. It is a good idea to write key words to your theme on the board. If you have a poster concerning your theme you could write the nouns that appear in the picture on 'Post-its' or separate small pieces of paper and stick them in the appropriate place on the picture with Blu-Tack. Show the children how they can remove the words, copy them and then replace them on the picture.

Year 1 children will still need counting aids to help them with simple mathematical calculations, but the older, Year 2, children should be encouraged to work independently.

It would be wise to prepare paints and glue in advance for this age group, but they should be able to find and put away general classroom equipment. Encourage them to wear aprons for messy work.

There will usually be construction and some table-top toys for this age group in the classroom. Year 1 and 2 children will not be used to doing academic-type work all day, but (as with Reception class children) avoid giving a 'free choice'; rather, limit the toys and where possible suggest activities.

Years 1 and 2 still enjoy picture stories but will also listen well to read-aloud stories without pictures. They prefer simple poetry to finger rhymes and probably consider themselves too old for nursery rhymes, but will enjoy singing simple, familiar songs.

These children enjoy themes to which they can relate their own personal experiences such as 'Homes', 'Birthdays' and 'Myself'.

Years 3 and 4

First and second year or lower juniors (Years 3 and 4) should be well adapted to school routine, although some Year 3 children may be a little unsure of themselves if this is their first term at a junior school. Children of this age should all be writing independently but they may welcome ideas on how to set out their work. It may be useful to have a few infant worksheets as you may find one or two children who need a lot of extra support. Some children may still have their own personal word books but most should be capable of using simple dictionaries and most will be fluent readers, but they will need some guidance if asked

to do reference work. They should be familiar with simple punctuation, but only the very mature Year 4 children will be attempting paragraphs and speech marks.

They should not need any counting aids at this stage, although they may well want to check their calculations on calculators.

These children are usually quite capable of getting their own materials out, but they still need supervision for certain experiments and for such subjects as woodwork. They should also know where to find things in the classroom and should be able to get PE apparatus out for themselves, but will need supervision.

They often seem to enjoy working on themes where they can use their imagination, such as 'Monsters' and 'Space'.

Years 5 and 6

Children in this age group used to be called third and fourth year (or top) juniors. They should be perfectly capable of organising themselves and any materials that they need, and should be confident about setting out their work and doing their own research. They can work well in groups. Top juniors can also use more difficult and dangerous classroom tools with supervision, such as glue guns, wall staplers and guillotines and are quite capable of doing their own mounting. They will also be confident in using dictionaries and some will be familiar with a thesaurus. Some of these children may be used to quite a degree of responsibility, such as helping to run a school bank or tuck shop, or putting out PE apparatus unsupervised, or helping younger children with reading or swimming.

They often respond well to topics relating to the world or environmental issues, such as 'Improving the world', 'Weather' or 'Newspapers'.

THE NATIONAL CURRICULUM

With the passing of the 1988 Education Reform Act, all state schools in England and Wales are required to follow the same curriculum for children aged 5 to 16. Scotland and Northern Ireland have their own curriculum guidelines, of which you will need to be aware in order to teach there. If you can, borrow some National Curriculum documents in order to become familiar with its complexities and jargon.

Glossary of National Curriculum terms

- AT: Attainment Target – the knowledge, skills and understanding which pupils will be expected and helped to acquire in one area of one subject as they progress through school.
- Continuous assessment: a teacher's on-going record of child's work.
- Core subjects: maths, English and science (and Welsh for Welsh-speaking schools in Wales).
- ERA: Education Reform Act 1988 – legislation which introduced the National Curriculum.
- Formative assessment: an assessment of the child's progress which informs teaching decisions about future learning.
- Foundation subjects: history, geography, technology, music, art, PE (Welsh for non-Welsh speaking schools in Wales) and a modern foreign language at secondary level.
- Key reporting stage: the end of one programme of study when SATs are administered; the stages are at 7, 11, 14 and 16 years of age.
- Key stages: the periods in each child's education to which the National Curriculum applies, i.e. Key Stage 1 (5–7 year olds), Key Stage 2 (7–11 year olds), Key Stage 3 (11–14 year olds) and Key Stage 4 (14–16 year olds).

- Level of Attainment: the ATs are divided into ten different levels of achievement.
- LMS: Local Management of Schools.
- Moderation: schools looking at each other's work and grading to achieve parity and consistency.
- Moderator: an external adviser specifically appointed to oversee any problems resulting from the moderation process.
- NC: National Curriculum.
- NCC: National Curriculum Council (see SEAC).
- Non-statutory guidance: advice for teachers on planning and implementing the NC (usually to be found at the back of NC documents.)
- Profile component (PC): groups of ATs brought together for ease of assessment and reporting.
- Programme of study: the matters, skills and processes which are to be taught at each key stage in each subject.
- SACRE: Standing Advisory Committee on Religious Education – advisory body for county guidelines on RE.
- SATs: Standard Assessment Tasks – externally prescribed set of standard tasks which pupils undertake in order to be assessed at the key reporting stages.

- Scheme of work: plan of work for each individual child to enable him/her to progress through the National Curriculum levels in each subject.
- SEAC: School Examinations and Assessment Council – oversees assessment of National Curriculum. (At time of printing, plans to merge SEAC and NCC were being developed.)
- Statement of attainment (SoA): more precise objective which is related to one of ten levels of attainment. Each AT is broken down into statements of attainment.
- Summative assessment: assessment used to provide a summary of achievement.
- TGAT: Task Group on Assessment and Testing.
- Weighting: the contribution which an individual AT makes to the final overall score. E.g., in the English SATs AT3 (Writing) has a higher weighting than AT4 (Spelling) and AT5 (Handwriting).

To sum up: each subject is divided into profile components (PC), which are made up of attainment targets (AT). Each attainment target is made up of more detailed statements of attainment (SoAs) (see Figure 1). Teachers are now required to make assessments against the statements of attainment and pupils are assessed at a level between 1 and 10 (see Figure 2).

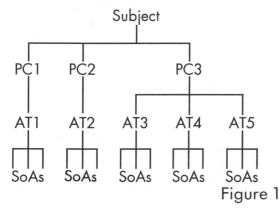

Figure 1

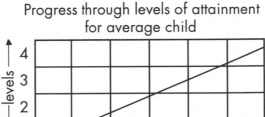
Progress through levels of attainment for average child

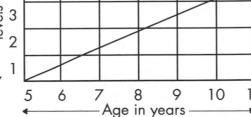

Figure 2

English
The English National Curriculum document does not state specifically how a child should be taught to read, but states that a child should be guided to 'build up a vocabulary of words recognised on sight; use available cues, such as pictures, contexts, phonic cues, word shapes and meaning of passage to decipher new words.' The teaching of reading varies from one school to another and it is better to fall in with the school's system.

If it is necessary to spell a word for a child, then the usual approach is to ask the child to make a rough attempt first. If this is incorrect, you should write the word and then ask the child to look at it carefully. The child should then cover it, write it and check it. Some teachers encourage children to complete their writing first and then go back and check their spellings. They may write words of which they are unsure as they think they are spelled and put a line under them or a ring around them or just write the initial letter of each word. You may be asked to give set 'spellings' or 'spelling tests'.

Some schools use joined handwriting from Reception. A quick glance around the walls will soon show you whether this is so. Also check the style of writing, for example whether certain letters have a loop at the bottom, e.g. 'l', and check how 'k', 's', 'y' and 't' are formed. You may be asked to give a formal handwriting lesson.

Drama
Drama activities, as well as featuring the programme of study for Speaking and Listening (English AT1), have many cross-curricular applications. Try, for instance, using drama for PE or history.

Mathematics

Much of the content of the Mathematics National Curriculum was already being taught, as standard, in most primary schools so you should have few difficulties here. Of the five ATs (Using and applying mathematics; Number; Algebra; Shape and space; and, Handling data), Algebra, as a new term at primary level, may cause some concern. However, its content is familiar: devising and exploring patterns and understanding that a symbol can stand for an unknown number.

Perhaps the one area where those who have been out of teaching for a while may be uncertain is in the use of calculators. In some schools, children are encouraged to use calculators from Reception. The National Curriculum states that children should be able to do calculations with and without calculators. Most schools encourage the children to work out their calculations mentally or on paper first and then to check their answers on a calculator.

You should be aware that some schools may not teach numerical operations in the way you have been taught. Others may prefer their pupils to devise their own methods of calculation. Therefore, it is better to avoid situations where you might feel it necessary to introduce a new method of calculation.

On the issue of 'tables', the National Curriculum states in AT2 Level 3 that children should be able to 'demonstrate that they know and can use multiplication tables.' (At Level 3 they should know the 2, 5 and 10 times tables and at Level 4 they should know all the times tables to 10.)

If you are planning to teach Year 6, it may be as well to revise π and the formulae for finding the areas of plane figures and the volumes of simple solids.

Science

If you have been out of teaching for some time you may well be concerned because science is now a core subject. If so, it would be wise to do a little background study particularly of electricity and magnetism, as pupils should have experience of using bulbs, buzzers, batteries and wire to investigate which materials conduct electricity.

Science also includes studying the development of the human body and a variety of animal and plant life, including extinct animals. It also involves studying materials and their properties and experimenting with melting, solidifying, dissolving and evaporation.

The children should also be observing the effects of weathering in their locality and be using measures to study weather conditions. Other areas covered by the curriculum include energy resources, energy transfer and forces and their effects. The children should investigate self-propulsion, motors, levers and gears. They will also look into pushing and pulling forces, gravity and the factors involved in sinking and floating.

Light and sound come into the curriculum too, requiring experiments with making sounds and investigating echoes, vibrations and pitch. They should also investigate shadows, reflections and the path of light and finally, research the motions of the earth, moon, sun and planets.

If possible, include some science teaching in your day. Check through the above list and see if any area might be covered through your chosen topic. It does not matter if you are not a science expert or if you feel you cannot give adequate explanations. The children will gain from making observations and making their own hypotheses.

Religious education

There are no National Curriculum documents for religious education, but each authority has been required to draw up its own guidelines. Most take into account the multi-cultural make-up of Britain while bearing in mind that the dominant religion is Christian. Some parents from certain faiths (and this includes some Christian denominations) will not allow their children to do any work associated with Christian religion. So even if you have planned to cover a Christian religious festival have some additional ideas ready for such children.

You may even be asked to do an instant assembly. The simplest thing to do is to read your planned story and try and draw out some moral threads from this. If you have brought any visual aids for your theme, it is also a good idea to show these. Finish with a prayer 'off the top of your head' about the subject.

History

History and geography are now important parts of the curriculum and should be included in your day's work wherever possible. Find out if your local museum education service is prepared to lend you items, and save postcards and birthday or Christmas cards with historical scenes on them. Another idea is to ask if the local studies department of the county library can lend or will allow you to photocopy photographs.

For infants, the National Curriculum suggests that they should be taught about everyday life in the past, introduced to a range of historical sources (such as artefacts, pictures and photographs, written sources and music) and cover the lives of some famous men and women and famous past events which are commemorated.

History at Key Stage 2 is probably the most prescriptive of all the National Curriculum areas and in some ways the most complex. The children have to study, over four years, a number of prescribed historical periods (such as Invaders and settlers, Tudors and Stuarts, Victorian Britain and Britain since 1930), covering themes such as food and farming, ships and seafarers and writing and printing.

From a supply teaching point of view, it would be a good idea to read a current edition of *History in the National Curriculum* and to familiarise yourself with these topics, as you may well be asked to carry on with a particular historical project. If possible try and link the theme you are covering with the particular period the children are studying.

Geography

The geography National Curriculum is divided into five areas: geographical skills; knowledge and understanding of places; physical geography; human geography and environmental geography.

In developing geographical skills the children will be learning to use coordinates and make simple maps and learning fieldwork techniques such as using a compass. In extending their knowledge of places, the children will be studying their local area, a different locality in the UK, a locality in a developing country and a locality in an EEC country. It is useful to purchase a world map and to buy an Ordnance Survey map of your local area. You may also find it useful to save postcards and pictures of various places.

Physical geography will include the study of earthquakes, volcanoes, rivers, erosion and weather conditions.

In human geography the children will investigate the uses made of buildings and land, transport, goods and services and learn why population changes occur and compare transport networks.

Environmental geography consists of learning where common materials are obtained and considering ways to improve the environment. Older pupils will also be taught the differences between renewable and non-renewable resources and investigate pollution.

Technology

Technology is probably unfamiliar ground if you have been out of teaching since 1989. However, most of it is straightforward and involves the development of children's abilities to find practical solutions to problems. Technology is about identifying needs and opportunities for improving the interaction of humans with their environment; about designing, planning and making things which fulfil a purpose; and about evaluating and assessing their own products and those of others, including those of other cultures and times. It involves both the development of problem-solving skills and specific knowledge skills of materials and technologies.

Information technology

Information technology is included as a distinct area of technology and is about presenting, storing and processing information by electronic means. It includes studying equipment such as toys and domestic appliances which respond to signals and commands. However, most of the content of the National Curriculum document is about using computers.

Computers

Most primary classrooms now have a computer in them and all children in state schools in England and Wales should have access to computers as a requirement of the National Curriculum. The children are, generally, familiar with how to operate the class computer and keen to use it. Try and familiarise yourself with these machines, either by going on courses or by asking a colleague or an articulate, enthusiastic top junior to show you. Do let the children use the computer: check whether there is a rota and, where possible, be specific about what they are to do, otherwise they will end up playing games. Children enjoy typing up their written work on the computer and printing this off. Encourage a variety of activities such as experimenting with pattern making, shapes and fonts, or have an on-going class activity such as collecting data for the day's theme or a continuous story.

Beware of the class computer 'buff' or 'expert' who will migrate towards the computer at every possible opportunity, claiming that whoever is on needs help!

Figure 3 shows a typical primary class computer system.

Most schools will have at least one printer and some will have a colour printer. If the computers are on a 'network' then you can check on the computer in the classroom whether the printer is free. If so, you will need to send the children to the location of the printer. If you are lucky enough to have a printer at hand, then just check the machines are connected and switched on and the instructions should come up on the screen.

Some infant classrooms may have a concept keyboard attached to the computer. This device has a series of overlays which are placed on a large tray. The overlays will be divided into about 20 sections and each section will have a word or picture printed in it. The children press these words or pictures which come up on screen as words which can be used to make sentences.

The children may also have access to a turtle or similar battery-operated, remote-controlled, programmable toy. The children key in their instructions first on the turtle's control panel.

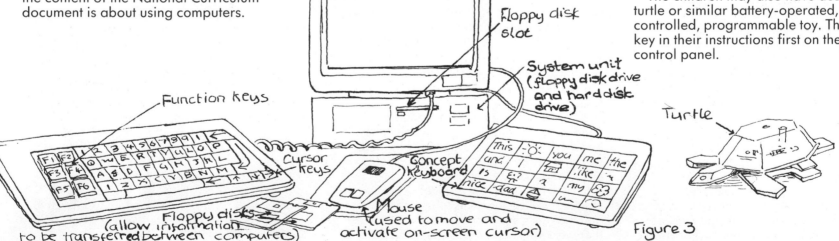

Figure 3

14

Art

The National Curriculum guidelines now emphasise not only personal creativity, but also the appreciation and evaluation of the works of established artists. Try to use artistic representations among your visual aids and encourage the children to analyse them critically for style and bias. Encourage the children to record direct observation as well as responding to memory and imagination.

On your first visit to a class it is probably wise to avoid having a number of 'messy' activities going on, and gradually introduce them as you become more familiar with the class and the equipment. Check whether the children are used to wearing painting overalls for specific work.

Physical Education

At Key Stages 1 and 2 the National Curriculum for physical education is divided into areas: gymnastics, games, athletics, dance, outdoor activities and swimming.

Although the children must be taught to swim 25m by the end of Key Stage 2, schools are free to choose whether to teach swimming at Key Stage 1 or 2 or across both key stages. The local authority requirements with respect to swimming teaching and life saving certificates vary regionally, so check whether you are suitably qualified. If you are very unhappy about the prospect of teaching swimming let the headteacher know, so that a lesson swop can be arranged. Also new, is the National Curriculum requirement for children to experience outdoor and adventurous activities in different environments and to undertake simple orientation activities.

For the other areas try and avoid using a lot of equipment or the apparatus on your first visit. If you are using the apparatus for the first time, ask another member of staff to make a safety check (you may have overlooked something). Some schools will insist that you change into a tracksuit and trainers for PE. If you are in a school with a very small hall, it may be safer to have only half the children active at one time with the rest watching. It is useful to learn the basic rules for netball, rounders and football, so that you can take a formal games lesson. Children also enjoy learning new games. You should always start your lessons with a few warm-up exercises and finish with some relaxing 'wind-down' ones. Since dance is also part of the curriculum, buy or borrow a folk dancing tape; the children will enjoy the novelty. Older children enjoy interpreting carefully selected pop music.

Music

As with art, the National Curriculum for music encourages both creativity and critical appreciation. As well as singing and playing, the children should be encouraged to record and perform their own compositions. If you are musical, use your talents; most schools will really appreciate this. A guitar is an ideal instrument; most children respond well to it and you can maintain eye contact as you play. It is worthwhile learning to play the guitar as many simple songs are covered by about a

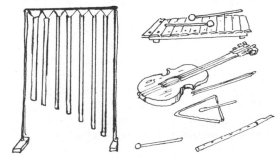

dozen chords. Make good use of the school's percussion instruments. Purchase one or two tapes of children's songs. If possible, buy some light classical music tapes to introduce the children to some well-known composers and music from different times, cultures and styles. The children will also be learning to distinguish different instruments and understand elements such as pitch and pace.

USING THE THEMES

The themes in this book are divided into four groups: Reception, Years 1 and 2, Years 3 and 4 and Years 5 and 6. Each theme covers a two page spread and the ideas are arranged under subject headings, with the three core National Curriculum subjects (English, maths and science) first, followed by the foundation subjects when appropriate. The 'What you need' section of each spread lists all the essential requirements for those ideas, while the 'Useful references' suggests stories, poems or background material with which to vary the day. Suggestions such as recommended song books and sources of additional materials and addresses from which they can be obtained are given in Part 3 'Reproducible material and resources' at the back of the book.

The book is designed for you to select the ideas which appeal and organise the work accordingly. Some teachers prefer to have all the children doing the same work at once, while others prefer a variety of activities to be carried out on the same subject. Some teachers may prefer to work an integrated day (with the children working on many different aspects of the curriculum at the same time). It depends on personal preference and the situation you may find yourself in.

For example, you may be told that you can only use the activity or art area at a certain time, or you may find yourself team teaching and be asked to cover a specific aspect of the curriculum with a group of children. Other schools have set timetables and it is best, wherever possible, to keep to these.

All the ideas in this book have been tried out and work with the suggested age group. However, you may find extremes of ability in your class and you would then have to simplify or extend the work accordingly. It should be possible to complete each idea in a day and, therefore, there are no suggestions for on-going activities (such as planting seeds or making large, elaborate models). Most of the suggestions for creative work are small and portable, so the children can take their objects home. The vast majority of the activities are to be done on an individual basis, but if this is not the case, then the text indicates whether it is a class or group activity.

It would be impossible to cover all the ideas suggested for a theme in one day. The intention is for you to 'dip in' and select those ideas which you think are the most appropriate and manageable.

'Instant' themes

The last three themes in each year group are particularly useful if you find yourself totally unprepared for the class you are about to teach. You may be asked to take a new age group or you might find the children have recently covered most of the ideas you had planned. These ideas will also be useful for a class teacher who is asked to take over another class for the day without any warning. Headteachers may also find this useful if they need to cover a class if a colleague is ill and a replacement cannot be found. The ideas can be carried out with the minimum amount of equipment and materials. Where materials are needed, they are usually to be found in most schools.

As before, the aim should be to cover a few of the ideas in a day. Some themes can be based around a single activity. For example, the children could base all their activities around a clock as in the 'Time' theme, or the class could work together to produce a class newspaper as in the 'Newspapers' theme.

If you do find yourself 'thrown in at the deep end', it is a good idea to explain what has happened to the children and enlist their help in getting out materials and collecting relevant books from the school library.

Although you will probably feel it, try and avoid being flustered and irritated. As a supply teacher you have to be prepared for the unexpected and to be adaptable. It is a good idea to memorise some of the following ideas and have a few more 'stand-bys' available in case you have to make some instant plans.

The hardest situation is if you are also asked to carry on with a particular theme and no specific work is set. Again, it is preferable to explain the situation to the class and there are some ideas listed below which may help.

English
Infants
Ask the children to draw a large shape associated with the theme and fill or surround it with words connected with that theme.

Make a concertina type book by fan-folding a piece of A4 paper. Ask the children to draw pictures on each fold to do with the theme. These can then be labelled by you or the children.

Juniors
Try an acrostic poem, word chain (see Years 3 and 4 'Patterns' instant theme) or step-word pattern (e.g., pig, goat, toad and so on). Suggest that the children write a newspaper-style report on the class activities on the theme. Ask the children to list and classify all the books they can find on the chosen subject.

Maths
Infants
Draw something connected with the theme using flat geometrical shapes. Make a simple chart of the children's likes associated with the theme.

Juniors
As above, but make individual bar charts or pie charts instead of a simple class chart. Work out how much time has been spent on the theme.

Art and craft
Infants
Ask the children to make a wax-resistant picture associated with the theme, painting watery colour over a wax-crayon drawing. If there are any catalogues in the room, the children could cut out a person and draw a background appropriate to the theme and stick on the figure.

Juniors
Ask the children to make a poster by writing a significant word in large print and adding relevant sketches to the letters. They could write the word in various styles and experiment with different types of decoration.

Part 2 – themes

Reception

Seaside

What you need

Travel brochures, plain paper, pencils, coloured pencils or crayons, scissors, adhesive, cardboard, hole puncher and treasury tags or stapler; magnetic fishing game (commercial or home-made); sand trolley, small trays (e.g. polystyrene food containers); small stones or pebbles, balancing scales, small bricks and cubes, copies of photocopiable page 115; shells, seaweed, whelk's egg case and other seaside items, pictures of sea life; objects of different materials, water trolley or bowl of water; pictures of old-fashioned bathing costumes and bathing huts; globe; powder paint (blues, dark green, grey and white), thick cardboard, blue sugar paper; green, white, blue and grey sugar paper, adhesive; musical instruments.

English
Free writing

Ask the children to draw a picture of themselves by the sea on plain A4 paper and then write or copy a sentence about it. Alternatively, they could cut out a picture from a travel brochure. At a later stage these sheets could be fastened together with treasury tags or a stapler into a class book and a cardboard cover added.

Catching 'word' fish

Use an adapted, commercially produced magnetic fishing game or make your own with small, simple, cardboard fish shapes with a hole punched through the head and a paper clip fastened through the hole. Rods can be made using a small piece of dowelling with some string attached and a small magnet fastened to the string. Write a simple word on paper with a reusable adhesive on the back (e.g. 'Post-it' notes), so that these can be pealed off and the fish used again for a simple counting game. Place the fish in a box and let the children take it in turns to 'catch a fish'. If they catch one, they must read the word correctly in order to keep it. The child with the most fish at the end is the winner.

Sand letters

Fill some shallow trays with dry sand from the sand trolley. Let the children practice making letter shapes by running their fingers through the sand.

Maths
Weighing stones

Let the children experiment with weighing stones on scales. If you want a written record of their work, photocopy one sheet of photocopiable page 115. Add the title 'Weighing a stone' and write 'stone' after the word 'This' each time on the page. Then photocopy the number you require. Ask the children to complete the sheets by drawing on the stones and cubes.

Counting stones

Cut up a number of sheets of plain paper to roughly A6 size. On each piece put a number between 0 and 10. Ask the child to place the corresponding number of stones, shells or pebbles on each piece of paper.

Science
Seaside life

Show the children shells, seaweed, a whelk's egg case and pictures of seaside life and talk to them about these.

Floating and sinking
Give the children a selection of 'seaside' objects, such as shells, pebbles and seaweed. Let them find out which things float and which sink in water (use the class water trolley or a bowl full of water). As an extension, ask the children to think about what materials a boat could be made from. Get them to experiment with objects made from different materials (for example wood, metal, plastic and paper) to see which sink in water.

History
Show the children pictures of people in old-fashioned bathing costumes and bathing huts. Discuss how things have changed.

Geography
Talk to the children about how far away they live from the sea, how they could travel there and how often they go. Look at a globe to see how much of the world is covered in water. Explain that new lands were discovered by people in boats.

Art and craft
Comb 'sea' pictures
Mix up some thick powder paint in blues, dark green, grey and white. Have some ready-made cardboard combs cut from thick card (see Figure 1). Some children may want to make their own combs. Ask the children to cover a sheet of blue A4 sugar paper with a mixture of the colours and then, while the paint is still wet, comb through the paint with their cardboard combs.

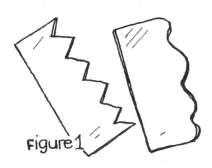

Figure 1

Wavy-strip patterns
Ask the children to cut out thin and thick wavy strips of blue, green, white and grey sugar paper. Show the children how to paste these overlapping horizontally on to a piece of blue sugar paper to give the effect of the sea.

Music
Let the children experiment with making 'sea' sounds with the musical instruments.

Songs
'The big ship sails through the Alley, Alley O' in *This Little Puffin*
'My ship sailed from China' and 'The train is a-coming' in *Apusskidu*
'I do like to be beside the seaside' in *Ta-ra-ra boom-de-ay*

Useful references
Information books
Spotter's Guide: Seashore S. Swallow (1978, Usborne)
Talkabout: Sand A. Webb (1986, Franklin Watts)
At the Seaside P. Lloyd (1990, Kingfisher)

Stories
Harry by the Sea G. Zion/M. Blay Graham (1966, Bodley Head)
Meg at Sea H. Nicoll/J. Pienkowski (1973, Heinemann/Picture Puffin)
Teddy: Teddy at the Seaside A. Davidson (1986, Armada)
Lucy and Tom at the Seaside S. Hughes (1992, Picture Puffin)
'The friend of the fisherman' in *Stories about Jesus the Friend* H. Rostron (1960, Ladybird)

Rhymes
'Here is the sea, the wavy sea' in *This little Puffin*
'There are big waves' in *The Young Puffin Book of Verse* (1970, Puffin)
'She sells sea shells on the sea shore' (Traditional)
'At the sea-side' in *A Child's Garden of Verses* R. L. Stevenson (1988, OUP)

Toys

What you need
Catalogues with pictures of toys in them, scissors, pencils, plain paper, rulers, adhesive; photocopiable page 116, coloured pencils; plastic circle shapes or small tissue paper circles; dice and shaker, counters or small bricks; dominoes; example of a 'big and little' sheet; table with a selection of toys, toy coins; large sheet of sugar paper, toy and gift catalogues; bath toys, water trolley; pictures of old fashioned toys; pictures of children from other countries playing with toys; card; paint, sugar-paper circles; assortment of types of paper, adhesive tape.

English
Toy-box
Show the children how to draw a simple toy-box outline in pencil on a sheet of plain paper (they could use a ruler for this). Ask them to cut out pictures of some of their favourite toys from catalogues and glue them on to the 'box'. The toys could then be labelled or a simple sentence written for the child to copy.

Like or dislike
Give each child a copy of photocopiable page 116. At the simplest level, ask the children to colour in the toys they like best. To make the activity more difficult, add the words 'yes' and 'no' at the top of the page. The children could then write 'yes' or 'no' alongside the pictures, depending on whether or not they like the toys shown.

   The children could be shown how to link up the toys with a common factor, by drawing a pencil line between them. The sets are: musical toys, outdoor toys and babies' toys. Alternatively, they could cut round the shapes and sort them into piles.

Maths
Counting balloons
Show the children how to draw round some small plastic circles shapes on a sheet of plain paper. Then draw a 'string' to each circle. The children could write the number of balloons they have drawn at the bottom of the sheet. Younger children could have tissue paper circles to stick on to the paper and add drawn 'strings' to these.

Dice game
This game is for a small group of children. The group will need dice, a shaker and a collection of small objects (such as counters, cubes or small bricks). The children take it in turns to throw the dice and pick up the correct number of objects. The winner is the one with the most objects, when they have all been picked up.

Dominoes
Let the children, individually or in pairs, join a long train of dominoes together by matching the spots. To extend this work, some children may be able to draw round a domino on a sheet of plain paper and then copy the spots.

Shopping
Put a selection of toys on a table. Ask one child to be the 'shopkeeper'. A small group of children can then pretend to buy toys using toy coins.

Science

Toys that need batteries
Write this heading on a large sheet of sugar paper. Ask a group of children to cut out from a toy or gift catalogue, pictures of toys that need batteries and glue them on to the paper.

Bath toys
Let the children play with some children's bath toys in the water trolley. Discuss why these toys float.

History
Show the children pictures of old-fashioned toys.

Geography
Find examples in the classroom of toys that are made in other countries. Show pictures of children from other countries playing with their toys.

RE
Encourage the children to consider how lucky they are to have toys to play with and to think about sharing their toys.

Art and craft
Ask the children to draw and colour in a picture on a piece of card. Ask them to cut the card into six 'jigsaw' pieces and then try to fit together each other's jigsaws.

Technology
Ask the children to make a paper bag in which to put their jigsaw pieces (see 'Art and craft' above). Encourage them to think about the size and shape of the paper bag and how it should be stuck together. They could use glue or adhesive tape.

Music
Listen to a short piece of the *Toy Symphony* (Haydn) or side one of the tape *Fun with Music: The Nutcracker* (EMI). Ask the children to guess what toys the music represents.

Songs
'Oh, we can play on the big bass drum' and 'Miss Polly' in *Okki-tokki-unga*
'Bananas in pyjamas' in *Apusskidu*
'See-saw, Margery Daw' in *The Nursery Rhyme Book*

Useful references
Stories
Teddy (series) A. Davidson (1985–, Armada)
Teddybears (series) S. Gretz (1983–, Hippo)
Peace At Last J. Murphy (1987, Macmillan Children's Books)
The Blue Balloon M. Inkpen (1989, Hodder and Stoughton)

Rhymes
'Round and round the garden', 'Here's a ball for baby' and 'Five little soldiers' in *Round and Round the Garden* S. Williams (1983, OUP)
'Rhymes and songs about toys' (chapter) in *This Little Puffin*

Food

What you need
Examples of fruit (including citrus), vegetables, a food packet and a tin of food or pictures of food, plain paper circles (about 14–18cm in diameter), plain paper, adhesive, pencils, coloured pencils or crayons, hole punch and treasury tags or stapler; photocopiable page 117; large cardboard clock with movable hands; brown sugar paper circles (about 6–8cm in diameter), scissors, cake fraction cards; four large sheets of sugar paper, magazines with food pictures; modelling material (Plasticine, clay or playdough); potatoes, sharp knife (for yourself), paint, saucers, sugar paper, newspaper; semi-circles of brown sugar paper (about 16cm in diameter), cotton wool; old yogurt pots, rice or lentils.

English
Favourite meal book
Have some pre-cut circle shapes in plain paper all the same size, about 14–18cm in diameter. Ask the children to draw their favourite meal on their 'plate'. Label their food for them to copy (or write over). Later, you could stick each plate on to a sheet of A4 paper, fasten the sheets together and add a cardboard cover to turn them into a book.

Fruit and vegetables
Give each child a copy of photocopiable page 117. Discuss the different foods with the children, explain that some are fruits and some are vegetables. If possible, show the children real examples of each food. Ask them to colour in the food they like. Alternatively, ask the children to colour all the fruit in one colour and all the vegetables in another.

Imaginative play
In the home corner suggest that the children pretend to be cooking and eating a meal.

Maths
Meal times
Discuss meal times with the whole class. Show these times on a large cardboard clock (limit this to o'clocks).

Cake fractions
Prepare some small circles (about 6–8cm in diameter), cut from brown sugar paper. Ask the children how they would share a 'cake' between two, then four. They could either draw lines on their 'cake' or cut it up. For extension work, have some simple prepared cards for the children to copy: on one card have a complete circle with the words '1 whole' written underneath; on another have two semi-circles with '2 halves' written underneath; on a third card have a circle cut into four with '4 quarters' written underneath (see Figure 1).

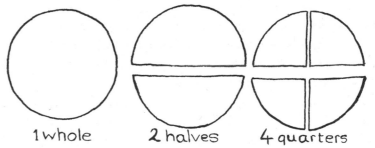

1 whole   2 halves   4 quarters

Figure 1

Count the fruit and vegetables
Photocopy one sheet of photocopiable page 117 and write the numbers 1 to 10 along the top. Then photocopy the number of these sheets you require. Ask the children to count and record the number of each item.

Science

Mark one of the following words: 'tins', 'packets', 'fresh food' and 'frozen food' on each of four large sheets of sugar paper. Stick a picture of each type of food on the appropriate sheet. Talk to the children about the way food is sold in the shops. Then ask the children to cut out pictures of food from magazines and glue them on to the appropriate sheet.

RE

Read or tell the story of 'The feeding of the five thousand' (John 6:1–5). Discuss food in other religions.

Geography

Tell the children about familiar food which is grown in other countries (such as bananas and citrus fruits).

History

Explain that we have had tins, packets and frozen food only recently. Ask the children to think about the kinds of food people would have eaten if they had to rely on keeping animals and growing food for themselves.

Art and craft
Food sculpture

Give the children some modelling material, such as Plasticine, clay or playdough and ask them to make some 'pretend' food.

Potato printing

Have some prepared potatoes, cut in half with a simple shape such as a cross or triangle cut from them (see Figure 2). Put thick powder paint in some saucers and show the children how to print on to sugar paper with the potatoes.

Ice-cream cornets

Prepare some semi-circles of brown sugar paper (about 16cm in diameter). Show the children how to form a cone from one of these and fasten it with adhesive or tape. Then ask the children to stuff the bottom of the cone with screwed up newspaper and glue some cotton wool on top of this so that it sticks out above the cone (see Figure 3).

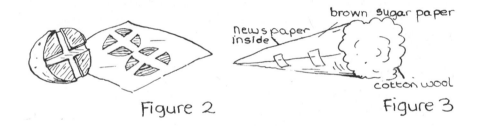

Figure 2　　　　　　　　　　Figure 3

Useful references
Stories

The Giant Jam Sandwich J. V. Lord/J. Burroway (1988, Piper Picture Books)
The Very Hungry Caterpillar E. Carle (1974, Picture Puffin)
The Doorbell Rang P. Hutchins (1986, Bodley Head)
The Tale of Mucky Mabel J. Willis/M. Chamberlain (1984, Andersen Press)

Rhymes

'Five fat peas' in *Round and Round the Garden* S. Williams (1983, OUP)
'Five currant buns in a baker's shop' in *This Little Puffin*
'The Queen of Hearts' in *The Nursery Rhyme Book*

Flowers

What you need
Selection of fresh flowers, pictures or posters of flowers; plain paper, pencils and crayons or coloured pencils; cardboard petals with words on, box or bag to put them in; large sheets of sugar paper, old flower or seed catalogues, adhesive, scissors; example of a 'tall and short flowers' sheet; flower vase with water; pictures of tropical plants; coloured tissue paper; old birthday cards or wallpaper; egg boxes, art straws, paint, crêpe paper.

English
Free writing
Ask the children to draw a picture of their favourite flower and write a sentence for the children to go over or copy.

Flower reading game
Cut out some small petal shapes of the same size from cardboard and write some simple words on them (see Figure 1). Put the petals in a box or bag and let the children take turns to take a petal out. If they can read the word, they keep the petal to make a flower. The winner is the child with most petals. This activity will need either an adult or a capable reader to supervise.

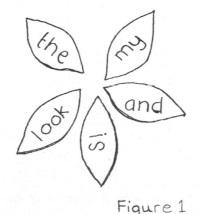

Figure 1

Maths
Sorting flowers by colour
Label some large sheets of sugar paper with different flower colours. Ask a group of children to cut out flowers from old flower and seed catalogues and glue them on to the appropriate sheet.

Tall and short flowers
Divide some sheets of plain A4 paper in half. On one side write 'tall' and on the other side write 'short'. Ask the children to draw appropriate flowers (see Figure 2).

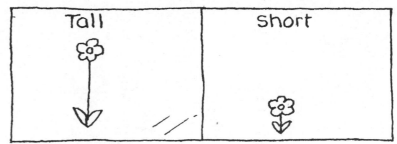

Figure 2

Science
Flowers need water
This will need to be done at the beginning of the day with the whole class. Bring in two flowers of the same variety. Explain that flowers need water to grow. Leave one flower without any water for the day and place the other in water. At the end of the day compare the two.

Looking at a flower
Show the children a flower and tell them the name of each part (such as stamen, pollen, petal, stem and leaves). Ask them to draw the flower carefully. Show the children how a bee can enter a flower to get honey. Explain that as the bee moves from flower to flower, it spreads the pollen so that the flowers can make seeds.

RE

Talk about the beauty of flowers and the pleasures they give. Tell the children about how flowers are part of worship for many people. Most Christian churches are decorated with them and they are used regularly in Sikh services. Buddhists have a ceremony where they float a lotus flower on a river or lake.

Geography

Show the children some real tropical plants or pictures of them. Discuss the kind of climate they need to grow (hot and wet).

History

Tell the story behind the song 'Ring-a-ring o' roses'. It originated during the time of the Plague in the mid-17th century, as sneezing was a first sign of the disease.

Art and craft

Tissue paper flowers

Have some pre-cut tissue paper circles of various sizes (see Figure 3). Show the children how they can 'fringe' the edge of the circles. Let them experiment with the tissue circles to make flowers. Show them how to place the circles on top of each other to make a flower. When they are satisfied help them to stick the flowers together.

Vases of flowers

Show the children how to draw simple vase shapes on plain paper and colour them in. Ask the children to cut some flowers from old birthday cards or old wallpaper and stick these on top of their vases (see Figure 4).

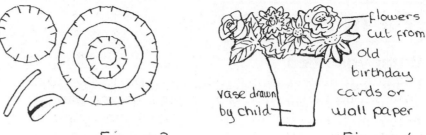

Figure 3

Figure 4

vase drawn by child

flowers cut from old birthday cards or wall paper

Technology

Give the children a selection of materials such as card, cardboard egg boxes, paper, crêpe paper, tissue paper and art straws and ask them to construct their own flowers.

Music

Songs

'Ring-a-ring o' roses', 'Mary, Mary quite contrary' and 'Here we go round the mulberry bush' in *The Nursery Rhyme Book*

''Neath the lilacs' in *Okki-tokki-unga* (First verse only and then change the word 'lilacs' for other flowers.)

'I like the flowers' in *Musical Fun with the Brownie Pack* H. Smith (1986, Girl Guide Association)

'All things bright and beautiful', 'Think of a world without any flowers', 'All the flowers are waking' and 'The flowers that grow in the garden' in *Someone's singing, Lord*

Useful references

Stories

Lucy Helps in the Garden R. Border (1985, Macdonald)
Titch P. Hutchins (1972, Picture Puffin)

Rhymes

'Round and round the garden' in *Round and Round the Garden* S. Williams (1983, OUP)
'Roses are red' in *The Nursery Rhyme Book*

Farm animals

What you need

Pictures of farm animals; photocopiable page 118, writing and coloured pencils; plain paper, cardboard, hole punch, treasury tags or stapler; toy farm, small cards with a number (1–10) on each; plastic or card shapes, toy animals; empty milk bottles, various containers, water, setting rings; large sheet of sugar paper, magazines, adhesive, scissors; cardboard sheep shapes, wool; Plasticine, clay or playdough; milk bottle tops, darning needle, cotton; empty milk bottles, water.

English
Farm animals

Give each child a copy of photocopiable page 118 and talk to the children about farm animals and their homes and products. Ask the children to draw a pencil line between each animal and its product and then each animal and its home. Ask them to colour in the pictures.

Farm animal book

Ask the children to draw one farm animal on a sheet of plain paper. Then write a sentence underneath for the child to copy or go over the top of the writing. Each sheet can then be joined to make a class book. A cardboard cover can be added later.

Maths
Toy farm

Most Reception classes have a class toy farm. Ask the children to put the same animals together. Ask them to sort the animals by colour and then by the number of legs.

To extend this work, label some small cards with a number from one to ten. Ask the children to place the correct cards by their sets of animals.

Shapes for animals' fields and pens

Show the children some plastic or card shapes (for example circle, triangle, square and rectangle) and tell them the name of each shape. Show them how to draw round each shape on a sheet of plain paper, imagining that they are fields or pens for the animals. They could then put one toy animal in each shape.

Capacity work using an empty milk bottle

Ask the children to fill an empty milk bottle with water, and tell them that this holds one pint. Pour the water from the milk bottle into other containers. Ask the children to find out which containers hold more, less or the same as the pint bottle. Put the containers into sets using setting rings. Take extra care when using glass bottles.

Counting and recording the animals' legs

Photocopy photocopiable page 118 once. Stick a strip of paper over the products and homes, so that just the animals show. Photocopy this for the number of children in the class. Ask the children to write '2' or '4' beside each animal depending on its number of legs.

Science
Ask the children which foods are made from milk. Write 'Things made from milk' at the top of a large sheet of sugar paper. Give the children some colour magazines and ask them to cut out pictures of foods made from milk. Stick the pictures on to the sugar paper to make a poster.

RE
Tell or read the story of St Francis of Assisi.

History
Recite some nursery rhymes which have children and farm animals in, such as 'Little Bo-Peep' and 'Little boy blue' in *The Nursery Rhyme Book* (1979, Wise Publications). Tell the class how young children were expected to look after farm animals in the past.

Art and craft
Woolly sheep
Prepare some simple sheep shapes cut from card. Show the children how to wrap white, grey, cream or black wool around the body part of the sheep (see Figure 1).

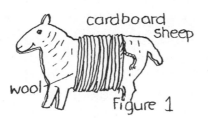
cardboard sheep
wool
Figure 1

Modelling animals
Provide the children with some modelling material such as Plasticine, clay or playdough. Ask them to make a farm animal.

Music
If you have a good collection of milk bottle tops, you could ask a few children to thread these on to strong cotton to make shakers. They will need adult supervision to do this, as it will require using a darning needle and cotton.

If you have a collection of empty milk bottles, fill them with different amounts of water and then tap them with a pencil to make different notes. You can demonstrate this with one milk bottle only by filling it to varying degrees and tapping each time. Take extra care when using glass bottles.

Songs
'Chicks grow into chickens' from *Scholastic Collections: Songs*
'Old MacDonald', 'The barnyard song', 'Baa, baa, black sheep', 'Mary had a little lamb' and 'The farmer in the dell' in *The Nursery Rhyme Book*

Useful references
Information Books
Understanding Farm Animals R. Thompson (1978, Usborne)
All About Farm Animals B. Cook (1988, Kingfisher Books)

Stories
Old Macdonald had a Farm P. Adams (1992, Child's Play International)
Rosie's Walk P. Hutchins (1992, J. MacRae)
Going to Sleep on the Farm W. Lewison/J. Wijngaard (1992, Andersen Press)
Is Anyone Home? R. Maris (1987, J. MacRae)

Rhymes
'This little pig' in *Round and Round the Garden* S. Williams (1983, OUP)
'Bow-wow, says the dog', 'I had a little pony' and 'Cock-a-doddle-doo' in *The Nursery Rhyme Book*
'The Farm' (chapter) in *This Little Puffin*

Easter

What you need

Pictures of Easter items; plain paper, pencils, coloured pencils or crayons, cardboard, stapler; photocopiable page 119, 6 egg boxes, 40 white and brown cardboard eggs; large piece of sugar paper, adhesive; Easter egg, cooking chocolate, Easter egg mould; white cardboard egg shapes, scraps of coloured sticky paper; tissue paper, strips of strong card; balls and skipping ropes.

English

Cut egg-shaped pages out of plain paper. Ask the children to each draw on their page a few things that they associate with Easter. You can then label these items and the children can copy or go over your writing. A cardboard cover can be made later.

Maths
Egg box number bonds

Give each child a copy of photocopiable page 119. In advance make a quantity of cardboard eggs (at least 40), approximately life-size, half in brown and half in white. Have available six empty egg boxes (of the half-dozen size) and ask the children, individually or in groups, to fill them with a mixture of brown and white cardboard eggs. They can then copy their egg box arrangement by colouring in on the photocopiable page the positions of the brown eggs with a brown crayon and leaving the white eggs blank. The children can carry on making other arrangements of eggs and copying them until their sheets are complete. You could dispense with the egg boxes and the cardboard eggs and let the children colour in the boxes with different combinations of brown and white eggs.

Our favourite eggs

Talk to the class about the variety of ways in which eggs can be cooked. Divide a large piece of sugar paper into five sections and write one of the following words into each section: 'boiled', 'fried', 'scrambled', 'poached' and 'omelettes'. Give each child a small piece of paper and ask them to draw and colour in pictures of their favourite kinds of cooked egg. Then, ask them to stick their pictures into the correct section of the chart. (This will need supervision.) When every child has completed an egg picture, total up the number of eggs in each section.

Science

Show the children an Easter egg, some cooking chocolate and, if possible, an Easter egg mould. Explain how the cooking chocolate is melted down and put into moulds to make an Easter egg.

RE

Read *The Easter Story* by J. Robertson (1979, Ladybird Bible Books/SU) and explain why Easter is an important festival for Christians.

History

Tell the children about some traditional Easter customs, such as wearing Easter bonnets on Easter Monday and egg rolling. There are historical details of such activities in *Bright Ideas: Easter Activities* by Jim Fitzsimmons (1988, Scholastic Publications).

Geography

Tell the children about Easter customs in other countries. For example, in Switzerland eggs are hidden all over the house in small baskets, while in Germany children have to search in the garden where the tradition is to hang eggs on an egg tree.

PE

It has been traditional to play ball and skipping games at Easter. In some parts of Oxfordshire, Easter Monday is still called 'Ball Monday'.

As well as practising simple ball skills, the children could try rolling the balls to simulate egg rolling. They could also play simple ball games such as 'Piggie in the middle'. Children of this age find it difficult to skip, but they might enjoy having the ropes out to try.

Art and craft
Easter egg mobile

Before the lesson cut out some egg shapes (various sizes) from white cardboard. Show the children how to draw a 'sash' across the centre of each egg on both sides. Ask them to colour in the egg on both sides in a plain colour with a thick crayon and use another crayon for the 'sash'. Then get the children to tear up some scraps of coloured sticky paper and stick these small pieces on to their egg (see Figure 1).

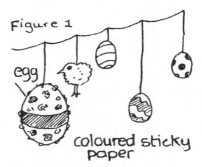

Figure 1

egg

coloured sticky paper

paper flowers

strip of strong card

tissue paper

Figure 2

Easter headband

Cut some strips of strong card (about 8×60cm) and ask the children to decorate these with paper flowers (see 'Flower' theme) and strips of tissue paper. When finished they can be stapled together to fit around a child's head (see Figure 2).

Music
Songs

'Hot cross buns' in *The Nursery Rhyme book*
'Entering Jerusalem' in *Scholastic Collections: Songs*
'Hurray for Jesus' and 'We have a king who rides a donkey' in *Someone's singing, Lord*

Useful references
Information books

Egg Poems J. Foster (ed.) (1991, OUP)
The Easter Book F. Trotman (ed.) (1987, Hippo)
Bright Ideas: Easter Activities J. Fitzsimmons (1988, Scholastic)
The Easter Book A. Farncombe (1984, NCEC)

Stories

Easter Bunny W. Wolf (1990, Beaver Books)
Meg's Eggs H. Nicoll/J. Pienkowski (1975, Picture Puffin)
The Great Big Especially Beautiful Easter Egg J. Stevenson (1984, Gollancz)

Rhymes

'Easter Eggs' in *Word Play Finger Play* S. Williams (ed.) (1984, PPA)
'Hickety, pickety, my black hen' in *The Nursery Rhyme Book*

Clothes

What you need

Pegs, washing-up bowl, washing line (or string); assorted buttons, large cardboard buttons; large wooden beads, laces; old clothes catalogues, scissors, plain paper, pencils, crayons, coloured pencils; sock, men's handkerchieves, tights, a flannel; sequins, small cardboard circles, safety pins or double-sided adhesive tape, cut-up straws, polystyrene loops and/or milk bottle tops; sugar paper, oddments of tissue paper.

English
Free writing

Ask the children to draw pictures of themselves wearing their favourite clothes. You can then write a sentence or phrase about each of their pictures for the children to copy or write over.

Imaginative play

In the home corner, suggest to the children that they dress up in a variety of clothes. They could also have a pretend washing day using a bowl, doll's clothes, washing line, pegs and a toy iron and ironing board.

Maths
Sorting buttons

Before the lesson make some large cardboard buttons with either two or four central spots drawn on them with a black felt-tipped pen. First, let the children look at an assortment of buttons and sort them by colour or size. Then, ask the children to count the holes in the real buttons and place them on the corresponding card button (see Figure 1).

Threading beads

Ask the children to thread beads on to a lace or string, first two of each colour, then three and so on, or the children could repeat a pattern which you have started.

Catalogue clothes washing line

Ask the children to cut out pictures of clothes from a catalogue. Then show them how to draw a washing line and stick the clothes on to the line. The children could count and record the number of clothes.

Comparing shoe sizes

Ask each child to draw round one of his or her shoes and cut it out. Help them to stick the cut-out shoes on to a class chart, comparing the sizes of shoes.

Science

Wet a number of men's handkerchieves and hang them in different places around the classroom. Ask the children to guess which one will dry first. They could put pieces of paper with their names on near the 'hanky' of their choice. Next, wet a sock, a handkerchief, a flannel and a pair of tights and hang them on a line. Again, ask the children to guess and then see which dries first.

Art and craft
A glove pattern

Show the children how to draw round their hands with their fingers outstretched. When they have done this, encourage them to design and colour in patterns for gloves.

Paper hats

Show the children how to make hats from sugar paper (crown and cone-shaped styles are the easiest for this age). The children could decorate their hats with scraps of tissue paper.

Jewellery

Show the children how to make necklaces by threading cut-up straws, milk bottle tops (with holes made in their centres using a pencil) or polystyrene loops on to strings.

You could also show them how to make a brooch by sticking sequins or tissue paper scraps on to a pre-cut, small cardboard circle. To attach the brooch, fix a safety pin or stick a piece of double-sided adhesive on the reverse.

History

Tell the children, with pictures if possible, about the clothes which people wore in the past.

Geography

Discuss with the children the kinds of clothes that people wear in other countries and show pictures of them.

RE

Talk about clothes worn in Bible lands and tell the story, 'Joseph and his coat of many colours' (Genesis 37).

Music
Songs

'This is the way we wash our clothes', sung to the tune of 'Here we go round the Mulberry bush'. Other verses might include: 'This is the way we wring/hang up/iron/wear our clothes'.
'Brrrr!' in *Scholastic Collections: Songs*
'My hat it has three corners' and 'My ship sailed from China' in *Okki-tokki-unga*

Useful references
Stories

Mrs Mopple's Washing Line A. Hewett (1970, Picture Puffin)
Mr Wolf's Week C. Hawkins (1987, Armada)
Alfie's Feet S. Hughes (1984, Armada)
You'll Soon Grow into Them Titch P. Hutchins (1985, Picture Puffin)
Two Shoes, New Shoes S. Hughes (1988, Walker Books)

Rhymes

'Grandma's spectacles' and 'Shoes' in *Round and Round the Garden* S. Williams (1983, OUP)

tissue paper sequins milk bottle tops beads cut-up straw

Preparing for Christmas

What you need

Pictures or posters of Christmas preparations; plain paper cut into stocking shapes, pencils, coloured pencils; old Christmas decorations, Christmas stockings, pillowcases, a sack; Christmas tree cards, counters; old cardboard boxes wrapped in Christmas paper, balancing scales, photcopiable page 115, cubes or bricks; four large pieces of sugar paper, gift catalogues, adhesive; old cardboard boxes, large sheets of kitchen paper, scissors, adhesive tape; wallpaper strips (16×3cm), adhesive; crêpe paper, empty toilet rolls; cardboard tubes, gold paper, paint, newspaper.

English
Christmas stockings

Give each child a Christmas stocking shape cut from plain A4 paper. Ask the children to draw what they would like to have for Christmas on their stockings. Label each item for the children to copy (or go over).

Imaginative play

In the home corner suggest to the children that they play 'Christmas Eve'. Give them Christmas stockings, pillowcases and a sack for one child to be 'Father Christmas'. Also, give them a bag of old Christmas decorations to decorate the home corner.

Maths
Christmas tree baubles

Make some simple Christmas tree shapes from A4 green card. Label each tree with a number between nought and ten (marked on the pot). Ask the children to put the correct number of counters (baubles) on the tree.

Weighing

Prepare some different-sized cardboard boxes wrapped in Christmas paper. Let the children experiment with weighing the parcels on some balancing scales. If you want a record, photocopy one sheet of photocopiable page 115. Add the title 'Weighing a Christmas parcel' and write 'parcel' after the word 'This' each time on the page. Then photocopy the number you require. Ask the children to record their results by drawing a parcel on the left-hand pan and then drawing the other objects they have used on the right-hand pan. They could either use single objects, building bricks or counting cubes.

Suitable presents

Get four large pieces of sugar paper and mark each with one word: 'Baby', 'Mum', 'Dad' or 'Children'. Ask a small group of children to cut out pictures from gift catalogues and stick them on the appropriate sheet.

Science

Discuss what a Christmas tree looks like, the type of tree it is, where it grows, the size it grows to and what it needs to grow. If possible, have a pine cone and a Christmas tree to show the children.

Technology

Find a selection of old cardboard boxes. Give the children some large sheets of kitchen paper and adhesive tape. Ask them to work individually or in pairs to wrap up the boxes without wasting paper.

RE

Read or tell the Nativity story (Luke: 1 & 2).

Art and craft
Wallpaper chains

Have a selection of pre-cut strips of different wallpaper about 16×3cm. Show the children how to make a paper chain by sticking the ends together and then passing the next strip through the loop (see Figure 1).

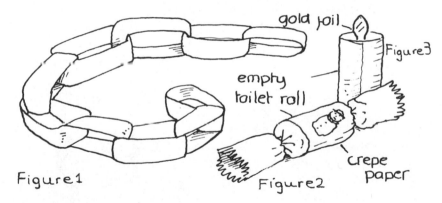

gold foil

Figure 3

empty toilet roll

Figure 1

Figure 2

crepe paper

Crackers

Cut some crêpe paper to A4 size. Show the children how to wrap one piece of paper around an empty toilet roll and twist the ends 'cracker fashion' (see Figure 2). The children could draw a funny picture on a small piece of paper to tuck into their cracker. They could also cut out small pictures from old Christmas cards and stick them on to the middle of the outside of their crackers.

Candles

Collect a selection of different-sized cardboard tubes and empty toilet rolls. Show the children how to cut a flame shape from a small piece of gold foil (or they could draw and colour in their own flame). Then ask them to paint their cardboard roll (see Figure 3). Alternatively, cover the toilet roll with white or coloured paper. Turn it into a 'candle' by pushing some screwed up newspaper into the top and gluing in the 'flame'.

Music

Listen to the first part of *Fun with music: The Nutcracker* (EMI) *Music*.

Songs

'Jingle bells', 'Oh, Christmas tree' and 'Away in a manger' in *The Nursery Rhyme Book*
'Ring bells, ring' in *Scholastic Collections: Songs*
'Rocking (Little Jesus sweetly sleep)' in *The Oxford Book of Carols* I. Elloway (ed.) (1988, OUP)
Many others in *Carol, Gaily Carol: A very unusual carol book* D. Gadsby/I. Gosby (eds.) (1985, A&C Black)

Useful references
Information books

Bright Ideas for Early Years: Christmas art and craft J. Fitzsimmons/R. Whiteford (1992, Scholastic)
Maths for Christmas (1988, Triad)

Stories

Lucy and Tom's Christmas S. Hughes (1989, Picture Puffin)
The Silver Christmas Tree P. Hutchins (1974, Bodley Head)
The Nativity Play N. Butterworth/M. Inkpen (1985, Hodder and Stoughton)
Mog's Christmas J. Kerr (1976, Collins)
The First Christmas L. Bradbury (1984, Ladybird Books)

Rhymes

'Christmas is coming' in *The Nursery Rhyme Book*

Butterflies

What you need

Pictures of butterflies and caterpillars; plain paper, pencils, coloured pencils or crayons; plastic shapes; gardening catalogues, black felt-tipped pens, adhesive; coffee filter-papers, felt-tipped pens, saucer, water, scissors; egg boxes, pipe cleaners; A3 sugar paper, poster paint; cardboard, various types of paper.

English

Ask the children to draw a picture of a butterfly and then copy a sentence about it.

Maths

Shape caterpillars

Show the children how to draw round plastic shapes on plain paper to make a horizontal caterpillar shape (see Figure 1).

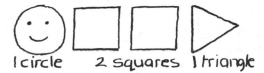

1 circle   2 squares   1 triangle

Figure 1

Counting butterfly eggs

Ask the children to cut out pictures of flowers or plants from gardening catalogues and stick these on to plain A4 paper. Ask them to put a few black spots with a felt-tipped pen, to represent butterfly eggs, on each flower. Then help them to count the spots. Some children may be able to write the number of spots underneath each flower.

Science

Life cycle of a butterfly

At the beginning of the day show the children pictures of caterpillars and butterflies and tell them about the life cycle of a caterpillar.

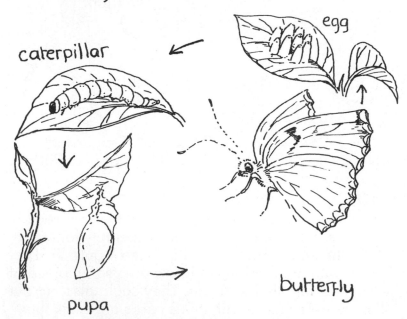

Butterfly life cycle.

egg

caterpillar

pupa

butterfly

Filter-paper butterflies

Ask the children to colour in coffee filter-papers with felt-tipped pens using horizontal lines and patches of colour. Tell them to colour from the narrowest point of the filter paper to about a third of the way up. Dip the bottom point of each filter-paper in a saucer of water and watch the water move up and the colours merge and spread. When dry, the filter paper can be cut open along the sides to reveal a butterfly with a symmetrical pattern on the wings (see Figure 2).

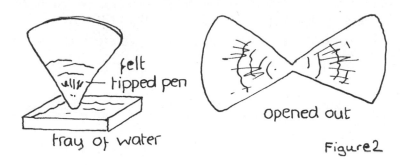

felt tipped pen

tray of water

opened out

Figure 2

Art and craft
Paper butterflies

Ask the children to fold a piece of A3 coloured sugar paper in half. Then show them how to draw half a butterfly shape (see Figure 3), and ask them to cut this out. Show the children how to put blobs of poster paint on to one half of their butterflies, then immediately fold the other half over and press gently. When the butterflies are opened out they will form a symmetrical pattern.

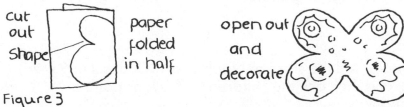

cut out shape

paper folded in half

open out and decorate

Figure 3

Egg box caterpillars

Before the lesson, cut up some large egg boxes into lengths of three or four sections each (or cut standard size boxes for six eggs, in half). Press two holes in each first section (see Figure 4), and show the children how to thread a pipe cleaner through and twist the ends to form antennae. Then ask the children to decorate their caterpillars using felt-tipped pens.

pipe cleaners

half an egg box

Figure 4

Technology

Give the children a variety of materials such as cardboard, various types of paper and adhesives and ask them to design their own butterfly or caterpillar.

Music

Listen to *Fun with Music: Mandy and the magic butterfly* (EMI).

Songs

'I went to the cabbages' in *Tinder-box: 66 songs for children* S. Barratt/S. Hodge (eds.) (1982, A&C Black)
'Caterpillars only crawl' in *Harlequin: 44 songs round the year* D. Gadsby/B. Harrop (eds.) (1981, A&C Black)
'Caterpillar lullaby' in *Scholastic Collections: Songs*

Useful references
Stories
The Very Hungry Caterpillar E. Carle (1970, Hamish Hamilton)
If At First You Do Not See R. Brown (1982, Andersen Press)

Rhymes
'Little Arabella Miller' (Anon.)
'The tickling rhyme' (I. Serraillier) in *The Faber Book of Nursery Rhymes* (1989, Faber)
'The caterpillar' (C. Rossetti) in *The Young Puffin Book of Verse* B. Ireson (ed.) (1970, Puffin)

Instant themes

Colours

What you need

Plain paper, writing pencils, coloured pencils or crayons, stapler or hole punch and treasury tags, cardboard; photocopiable page 117; magazines or catalogues, scissors, adhesive, large sheets of sugar paper; different coloured cubes or bricks; beads and laces, pegs and pegboards; pre-cut large circles and triangles, a highway code book; washing-up liquid, powder paint, art straws, clean yogurt pots; cardboard, coloured transparent film.

English
Class colour book

Ask the children to choose one colour and then draw and colour in objects which are that colour. You could then label these objects and either ask the children to go over the top of your writing or copy underneath. The pages could later be made into a class book.

Colouring in food in the correct colours

Give each child a copy of photocopiable page 117 and ask them to colour in all the pictures in their correct colours using coloured pencils.

Pictures of one colour

If there are magazines or catalogues in the classroom, you could ask the children to cut out pictures of a particular colour and stick them on large sheets of sugar paper labelled with that colour.

Maths
Counting and sorting by colour

Ask the children to sort the coloured pencils or crayons by colour and then count how many there are of each colour. Ask the children of which colour there are the most coloured pencils and which the least. Other items such as bricks or cubes could also be sorted by colour and counted.

Copying a coloured pattern

Most reception classrooms have beads, cubes or pegs. Start the children off with a few threaded beads (or pegs on a board, or joined cubes) and ask the children to copy and repeat the pattern that you have started.

Science

If the weather is fine, and if the school has a suitable environment, take the children outside and ask them to pick a collection of leaves (only one per tree specimen) of different colours. The children could then mount their leaves on sugar paper.

RE

Read or tell the story of Noah's Ark (Genesis 6: 9 – 9: 17) and then ask the children to draw or paint a rainbow.

Geography

Cut out some white circles and triangles of paper or card. Explain that circular road signs with a red border must be obeyed, whereas triangular shapes are warning signs. Ask the children to draw and colour in with crayons the signs that they remember. Remind them to colour in a border (where appropriate) and to use only red, white, blue and black colours. They could use paint on pre-cut large sheets of sugar paper.

Art and craft
Bubble painting

Borrow some washing-up liquid from the school's kitchen (if possible). Mix a little of this with some powder paint and water in a clean yogurt pot or cup-like container. Then show the children how to blow through a straw so that the bubbles come to the top of the container. Quickly place a piece of sugar paper over the bubbles to form a print (see Figure 1). This will need supervision!

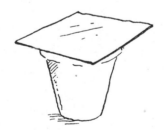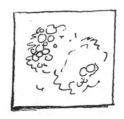

Figure 1

Mixing colours

Show the children how to draw round a large circle in the centre of a piece of sugar paper and then draw some smaller circles around this (or, alternatively, have some paper prepared like this already, Figure 2).

Prepare some powder paints and have some mixing trays handy. Then ask the children to choose a colour and paint the centre circle in this. Then they should mix a little of their main colour with another colour in the mixing tray and paint one of the outer circles in this. They should do the same for the other circles, but always using their main colour mixed with another.

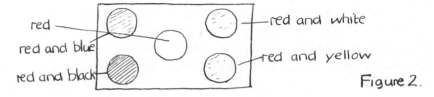

Figure 2.

Technology

Ask the children to design a pair of glasses using cardboard, coloured transparent film and adhesives of their choice. Warn the children that, even when wearing tinted glasses, they should never look directly at the sun.

Music
Songs

'Sing a rainbow' in *Apusskidu*
'Little Boy Blue' and 'Bobby Shaftoe' in *The Nursery Rhyme Book*
'Colours' in *Scholastic Collections: Songs*

Useful references
Stories

The Mixed-up Chameleon E. Carle (1988, Picture Puffin)
Colours S. Hughes (1986, Walker Books)
The Blue Balloon M. Inkpen (1989, Hodder & Stoughton)
Spot Looks at Colours E. Hill (1986, Heinemann)
Colours J. Pienkowski (1974, Heinemann)
The Amazing Story of Noah's Ark M. Williams (1990, Walker Books)

Poetry

Hailstones and Halibut Bones M. O'Neil (1962, World's Work)

Myself

What you need
Plain paper, writing pencils, coloured pencils, crayons, yellow felt-tipped pen, sand, trays; small pieces of card; magazines, catalogues or photocopiable pages 116 and 117, scissors, adhesive; self-adhesive labels (e.g. 'Post-its') or Blu-Tack; cubes; paint, sugar paper, saucers or shallow containers; circles of white card or white sugar paper, wool (optional); Plasticine, clay or playdough.

English
Writing their own names
Ask the children to write their names in a variety of colours, using both pencils and crayons. For those who are unable to write their own names, write them in yellow felt-tipped pen and ask the children to go over the top of this and/or encourage them to copy underneath. An extension of this could be to fill some trays with sand from the sand tray and ask the children to write their names in the sand; alternatively, encourage them to do this when they are playing in the sand tray.

Things I like
If there are any magazines or catalogues in the classroom, ask the children to cut out a few pictures of things they like and paste them on to a sheet of paper. Alternatively, give the children copies of photocopiable pages 116 and 117 and ask them to cut them up but colour in the pictures as well.

Maths
Measuring their heights
Ask the children to write their name on a self-adhesive label or 'Post-it' (cut off the non-adhesive part). Then ask each child to stand in turn against a door or unused wall and mark his or her height with the label. (Either you or a helper will need to do this or the children could work in pairs.) Alternatively, use strips of paper with Blu-Tack on the back. The children could also find and draw something which is taller than themselves and something shorter.

Joining cubes
Ask the children to join cubes together to make the row a similar length as their longest fingers, then their hand spans and finally their arms. They could compare their rows with those of other children (see Figure 1).

Figure 1

Science
Our hands
Get the children to study their hands and point out finger nails, knuckles and veins. Then ask the children to draw round one hand and put in these features.

How we change
Have a class discussion on how we develop from a baby, through childhood to adults and old age. Ask the children to find pictures in story-books of the different stages of human development.

RE

Pool the children's ideas on how to help each other and challenge them all to do something to help someone else by the end of the school day. Go over what they have done in the last session.

History

Encourage the children to talk about their grandparents, concentrating on the things they said they did when they were children. Then ask the children to draw their families including all their grandparents. What things have changed since their grandparents were children?

Art and craft

Thumb pots

Demonstrate how to make a ball out of modelling medium such as Plasticine, clay or playdough; and then push your thumb in the centre to make a thumb pot. Invite the children to do likewise (see Figure 2).

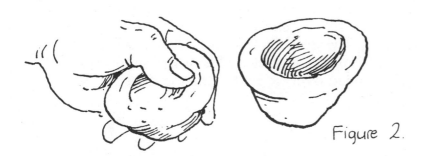

Figure 2.

Cardboard faces

Cut out some circles of white card or sugar paper. Then ask the children to draw on to a card a picture of their own face. If you can find some wool, encourage the children to add this for hair.

Finger painting

Mix some paint up in saucers or shallow containers. Then ask the children to dip their fingers in the paint and make a pattern or picture on sugar paper.

PE

Warm up by shaking or rubbing different parts of the body in turn. Then concentrate on feet and different ways of jumping, running, hopping and walking (include 'tiptoes', stamping and walking on heels). Move on to crawling and 'bunny hops' and finally to backs and tummies and rolling. Finish the lesson with some tag games and wind down with lying down and relaxing each part of the body in turn.

Music

Find out if the children have a favourite school tape. Borrow this and the school's tape-recorder. Then, while the tape is playing, beat out the rhythm by tapping different parts of your body and marching on the spot.

Songs

'Heads, shoulders, knees and toes', 'Join in the game', 'Everybody do this', 'Do your ears hang low?', 'Put your finger on your head' and 'One finger, one thumb, keep moving' in *Okki-tokki-unga*
'If you're happy . . .' in *Apusskidu*

Useful references

Stories

Just Like Me J. Ormerod (1989, Walker Books)
Titch P. Hutchins (1972, Picture Puffin)
Trouble with Dad B. Cole (1987, Armada)
Oscar Got the Blame T. Ross (1987, Andersen Press)

Shapes

What you need

Plain paper, writing pencils; stapler or hole punch and treasury tags, cardboard; rulers, selection of various kinds of papers, scissors, adhesive, large sheet of sugar paper; flat shapes, coloured sugar paper, felt-tipped pen, bag; computer, drawing program; 3D shapes; bricks; globe; paint; 'junk' materials; PE mats.

English
Word shapes

Write some simple words such as 'I', 'am', 'mum', 'dad', 'a', 'and', 'like' and 'my' on a piece of plain paper. Draw around these words (see Figure 1) and then place four or five pieces of paper behind this and cut out the shapes altogether. Then ask the children to match the shape with the correct word.

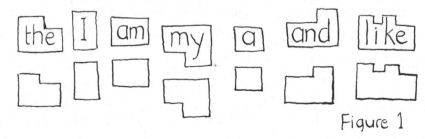

Figure 1

Shape book

Ask each child to choose a shape (such as a square, rectangle, triangle or circle) and draw things which are only that shape. You could then label the objects and let the children copy or go over your writing. A class book could be made by joining the pages together and adding a cardboard cover later.

Maths
Making triangles

Explain that a triangle always has three sides and then ask the children to draw triangles of various sizes using rulers and pencils. Alternatively, give the children a selection of papers (for example sugar paper, coloured paper and magazine pages) and ask them to draw and cut out their triangles. These could be stuck on a large sheet of sugar paper.

Simple shape game

If you have access to a box of flat shapes, note the colours and find some similar coloured sugar paper. Ask the children to choose a colour and draw around a square, rectangle, triangle and circle of that colour in felt-tipped pen on to a sheet of coloured sugar paper (see Figure 2). When the children have finished ask them to place their shapes in one empty PE bag.

The game is played with each child having one of the different-coloured sheets of sugar paper. They each dip into the bag in turn and draw out a shape. If it is the same colour as their sheet they cover the appropriate drawing with the shape. If not, they return the shape to the bag. The game is finished when one child has covered all the shapes on his or her sheet. The game can be used over again by other children.

Figure 2.

Computer shapes

Ask the children using the computer to make some shapes using a drawing program. They should experiment with colouring, enlarging, repeating and reversing (depending on the capabilities of the computer).

Science

Give the children a selection of 3D and flat shapes. Ask them to find out which ones roll. Ask the children to fold a piece of paper in half and on one side draw the shapes that roll, and on the other side the ones that do not roll.

RE

Ask the children if they know why the cross shape is important to Christians and then discuss this.

Geography

Show the children a globe and explain that it is a sphere. Point out Britain and other countries of which the children have heard.

Art and craft
Making pictures from shapes

Ask the children to draw around flat shapes and make a picture from these. This could then be coloured in (see Figure 3). Shape people could be drawn similarly by adding a face in the centre and arms and legs.

Figure 3

Printing with shapes

Collect items from around the classroom, such as LEGO or Duplo bricks, cotton reels, lids, empty containers and some 3D shapes. Cut up some sugar paper into large circles, squares and rectangles. Mix up some thick paint on saucers or shallow containers and then show the children how to print with the collected objects.

Technology

If there are plenty of 'junk' modelling materials, ask the children to make something, but ask them to restrict their construction to using only one 3D shape.

PE

The lesson could revolve around the children making shapes with their bodies. They could draw shapes in the air with their arms and make themselves into round, long, wide, narrow, short, tall and crooked shapes. Get the mats out and let the children experiment with moving in these shapes (such as rolling like a ball). Then let them work in pairs to make shapes together, and finally let them work in small groups.

Useful references
Information books
All Shapes and Sizes S. Hughes (1986, Walker Books)
Colours and Shapes L. Bradbury (1981, Ladybird Books)

Stories
Arabella: The smallest girl in the world M. Fox (1986, Hippo)
The Blue Balloon M. Inkpen (1989, Hodder and Stoughton)
Mr Strong; Mr Happy; Mr Rush and *Mr Grumpy* R. Hargreaves (1990–1, The Mr Men Own Stories/World International Publishers)

Years 1 and 2

Autumn festivals

What you need
Harvest festival gifts, pictures of a harvest festival, plain paper, writing pencils, coloured pencils; photocopiable page 117, loaf of sliced bread, 1cm squared paper, Multilink or Unifix cubes; magazines, scissors, adhesive, large sheet of sugar paper; apples, knife; hole punch and treasury tags or stapler, pictures of different 'thank you' festivals; A5 sugar paper, rulers, scissors, flower catalogues; example of Pearly King outfit, black sugar paper, rounded sticks, thick white paint; processional music.

English
Harvest festival box
Discuss with the children the reasons for holding harvest or autumn thanksgiving festivals. If possible show a picture or bring some examples of the kind of food and goods brought to a harvest festival. Then ask the children to draw a simple basket and fill it with things they would like to take to a harvest celebration and write about them (see Figure 1).

Fruit and vegetables
Make a photocopy of photocopiable page 117. Write the names of all the fruit and vegetables across the top of the page, then photocopy the number you require. Ask the children to put the correct name under each food. Year 2 children should be able to write a simple sentence underneath each food item.

Maths
Area of a slice of bread
Bring in a loaf of sliced bread and give each child a slice. Ask them to draw round their slices on 1cm squared paper and then count the number of squares that their slice covers and record this underneath. Next ask the children to estimate how many cubes (Multilink or Unifix) would go round the edge of their slice, and then find out and record.

The cost of a festival
Ask a group of children to cut out pictures from magazines of things they think might be needed for a festival and to stick these on to one large sheet of sugar paper. Give each item a price (no more than 20p). Then ask the children to make a short list of the things they would like to buy (for Year 1 limit this to two items unless very competent). Help them to write down the prices and total this up to see how much their choices would cost.

Figure 1

Science
Halved apples
Cut some apples in half and then ask the children to draw what they see.

Where things grow
Have a class discussion about which foods grow above or below the ground. Then ask the children to list these foods under the headings 'Above the ground' and 'Below the ground'.

RE

Tell the children about different 'thank you' festivals for example, Sukkot (Jewish), Diwali (Sikh/Hindu) or Labour Thanksgiving Day (Japan). Then tell them to each write a 'thank you' poem, song or prayer about the things they most appreciate. These could be made into a book by adding a cardboard cover later.

History

Read or tell the story of the Pilgrim Fathers' voyage to America. Explain that Americans celebrate by having a Thanksgiving Day on the fourth Thursday in November which commemorates the Pilgrim Fathers' first harvest in America. Turkey and pumpkin pie are the traditional foods for this day.

Art and craft
Paper flower weaving

Show the children how to fold a piece of A5 sugar paper in half widthways and draw a line 3cm from the open edge, but parallel to this edge. Then draw lines 3cm apart from the fold to the first line and cut along these lines. Next show them how to measure and cut strips (3×18cm) from old flower catalogues and weave these in and out of the cut base (see Figure 2). (Year1 children could use a ruler's width in place of measuring the lines.) During the festival of Onan, in India, children weave flowers into mats.

Pearly King and Queen outfits

In London, Pearly Kings and Queens parade in costumes covered with buttons to mark harvest-time. Show the children how to fold some small pieces of black sugar paper in half and cut them to make clothes shapes (see Figure 3). Then dip a rounded stick (or the

unsharpened end of a pencil) in white paint and print circles on to the 'clothes' to represent the buttons. The children could draw people too and stick the clothes on to them.

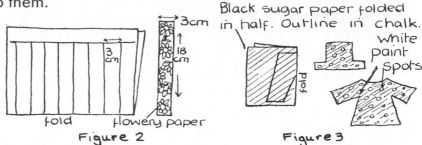

Figure 2

Figure 3

Music

Listen to some processional music, such as 'Arrival of the Queen of Sheba' from *Solomon* (Handel) or *Pomp and Circumstance Marches* (Elgar) or 'March' from *The Nutcracker Suite* (Tchaikowsky).

Songs

'A Ram Sam Sam' in *Flying A Round: 88 rounds and partner songs* D. Gadsby/B. Harrop (eds.) (1982, A&C Black)
'The farmer comes to scatter the seed' in *Someone's singing, Lord*
'Harvest' and 'Light up Diwali' in *Scholastic Collections: Songs*

Useful references
Information books
Bright Ideas: Festivals J. Bennett/A. Millar (1988, Scholastic)
Shap Calendar of Religious Festivals (annual, Hobsons)

Stories
The Little Red Hen V. Southgate (1986, Ladybird)
Deep in the Dark Wood P. Blakely (1982, A&C Black)

Poetry
Let's Celebrate: Festival poems J. Foster (ed.) (1989, OUP)

Birds

What you need

Christmas and birthday cards or magazines with pictures of birds, plain paper, pencils, adhesive; board and chalk, books about birds; pictures of talking birds, coloured pencils; calculators or counting materials; small pieces of plain paper, large sheet of sugar paper; cooking oil, water, large container; scissors, black ink; globe or world map; example of bird mobile, cardboard, scissors, coloured paper, cotton; brown sugar paper, black felt-tipped pens, brown and white tissue paper, adhesive tape.

English
Descriptive writing

Let the children choose a picture of a bird from an old Christmas or birthday card or magazine. Ask them to describe the bird by writing about its colours, beak, size and where it might live. Ask the children either to copy pictures of their chosen birds to go with their writing or to stick their pictures underneath their writing.

Talking birds

If possible, have some pictures of parrots or other talking birds and ask the children to draw them. Discuss the kind of amusing things that a talking bird might say. Show the children how to draw a speech balloon above their bird and write in it something the bird might say.

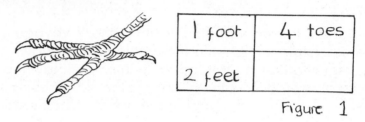

Maths
Birds' claws

Draw a bird's foot with four toes (see Figure 1) and write '1 foot 4 toes'. Then write underneath '2 feet' and ask the children to work out how many toes. Ask the children to copy and continue this for as many feet as they can. They could use calculators or counting materials to help them.

1 foot	4 toes
2 feet	

Figure 1

Categorising birds

Ask each child in the class to draw a picture of their favourite bird on a small plain piece of paper. Stick these on a large sheet of paper with the heading 'Our favourite birds'. Talk about the different ways we can classify birds by looking at their colour, beaks or size.

Science

Explain the word 'preening' to the class (the spreading of oil through the feathers from the oil gland near the tail). Show the children why water birds do not get wet, by putting some cooking oil on a feather and dipping it into water. Then add some oil to water in a container to show that oil and water do not mix.

History

Explain to the children that before pens were invented people wrote with quills and ink. If possible, let the children experiment with writing with feathers and black ink on plain paper.

Geography

Talk to the children about migration and show the children on a globe or world map where our visiting birds migrate to.

Art and craft
Bird mobiles

Show the children how to draw and cut out a simple bird profile from cardboard (or alternatively have some ready-made). Then ask them to make a fan out of coloured paper for the wings and slip this through a horizontal slot in the bird's profile. Decorate the birds and string them with cotton to make them into a mobile (see Figure 2).

Figure 2

Owls

Have some oval shapes of various sizes cut from brown sugar paper. Show the children how to draw on two large simple eyes and a triangular beak with a black felt-tipped pen and cut small triangles of brown or white tissue paper and stick these on to the owl as its feathers (see Figure 3).

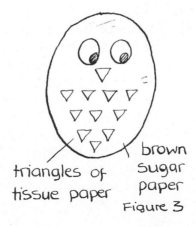

Figure 3

Music

Listen to 'The aviary', 'The swan' and 'The cuckoo' from *Carnival of the Animals* (Saint-Saëns) and 'The bird song' from *Peter and the Wolf* (Prokofiev).

Songs

'Kookaburra' in *Flying a Round: 88 rounds and partner songs* D. Gadsby/B. Harrop (1982, A&C Black)
'Sparrow twitters' in *Apusskidu*
'Cuckoo! Cuckoo!' in *Harlequin: 44 songs round the year* D. Gadsby/B. Harrop (1981, A&C Black)
'Six little ducks' in *Okki-toki-unga*
'Morning has broken' and 'A little tiny bird' in *Someone's singing, Lord* (1977, A&C Black)
'When the red, red robin' in *Ta-Ra-Ra Boom-De-Ay*
'Owl can't get to sleep' in *Scholastic Collections: Songs*

Useful references
Information books and packs

Early Birds: Ideas for bird studies for 5–8 year olds (1991, RSPB)
Amazing Worlds: Birds A. Parsons/J. Young (1990, Dorling Kindersley)
World Wildlife: Birds (1988, Ladybird/WWF)

Stories

The Ugly Duckling H. C. Anderson (1981, Award Publishers)
Penguin S. Jenkins-Pearce (1988, Hutchinson)
Have You Seen Birds? J. Oppenheim (1989, Hippo)
The Owl Who Was Afraid of the Dark J. Tomlinson (1992, Methuen)
Goodnight Owl P. Hutchins (1975, Picture Puffin)
Two Can Toucan D. McKee (1986, Beaver)
The Amazing Story of Noah's Ark M. Williams (1990, Walker)

Poetry

'Cage bird and sky bird' (L. Norris), 'The grasshopper and the bird' (J. Reeves), 'The owl and the pussy cat' (E. Lear) in *The Oxford Treasury of Children's Poems* M. Harrison/C. Stuart-Clark (1988, OUP).

Birthdays

What you need

Birthday cards, pencils, plain paper; board and chalk; coloured pencils; two large sheets of sugar paper sectioned into months, small pieces of plain paper; pretend coins; pictures of Victorian children; globe or world map; examples of birthday wrapping paper, paint, cardboard; 13 sheets of plain white paper, scissors; rulers; musical cassette.

English

Describe a birthday card

Bring in a selection of birthday cards. Ask the children to choose one and then write a description of the picture on the card.

Birthday poem

Read the class a selection of rhymes from birthday cards. Work out a simple rhyme verbally with the class. Challenge the children to make up a birthday rhyme of their own and write this down. For Year 1, you could write some words on the board for which they can find rhymes (such as 'day', 'boy', 'year' and 'sun').

Birthday invitation

Write on the board:
'Dear . . .
Please come to my (birthday) party on . . .
At . . . o'clock at my house.
Love from . . .'
Ask the children to copy this and fill in the blanks. Some children may be uncertain as to when their birthday is, so have the class register handy to check. Some children may be able to write their address instead of 'my house'.

Maths

Class birthday chart

Divide two large sheets of sugar paper into six sections and write the name of a month in each section. Explain the calendar to the class. Then ask the children to write their name and their birthday on a small piece of paper. Help them to stick their names in the appropriate month. When the chart is complete, record the number of birthdays in each month and compare the results.

Birthday shop

Collect some toys, books and games from around the classroom on to one table and include some old birthday cards. Explain to the class that this is an imaginary shop and write some price labels (limit this up to 20p) for the items. Ask the children to imagine that they are choosing a card and a present for a friend's birthday. Suggest that they go to the 'shop', select what they want and pay for it with pretend money. They could record what they have bought in pictures and writing, together with the prices and the total they have spent. You could show them on the board how to set this out. Let the children take it in turns to be shopkeepers.

Science

Explain that birthdays are a yearly celebration of the day that the children were born. Ask the children if any of them know where they were born. Find out if there has been a recent birth in any family and encourage the children to ask questions about the new arrival. Discuss what a child might be doing on each birthday up to the age of seven. The children could draw a picture of each stage, starting with 'Birth day', then '1st birthday', '2nd birthday' and so on.

'Happy Birthday banner'
each child makes a letter

Figure 1

RE

Explain that Christmas celebrates the birthday of Jesus. Tell the children that other faiths celebrate birthdays too, for example, Hindus celebrate Ganesh's birthday in September.

History

Tell the children that people who live to be 100 years old get a telegram from the Queen. Discuss what life was like 100 years ago for children, describing the kind of toys, clothes and schooling children would have had (with the help of pictures if possible).

Geography

Find out if any of the children receive birthday presents or cards from abroad. If so, look up these countries on a globe or map of the world.

Art and craft

Wrapping paper

Show the children examples of birthday wrapping paper. Ask them to design their own on A3 paper. They could try printing (see Years 1 and 2 'Patterns' theme). They could draw around shapes and paint these, or make a simple cardboard template for a repeat pattern.

Birthday banner

Give 13 children a sheet of plain white paper each and specify a letter for each child from 'HAPPY BIRTHDAY'. Show the children how you want the letters to be drawn and ask them to make a bright pattern inside with crayons. Cut out the letters and stick them in the correct order on a long strip of paper (see Figure 1).

Technology

Challenge the children to make their own pop-up birthday card. Show them a ready-made example of this (see Figure 2).

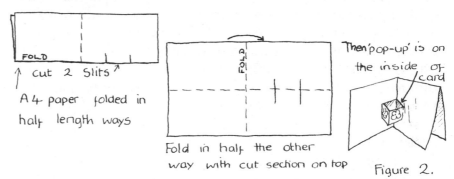

Figure 2.

PE

Ask the children to imagine they are at a birthday party. With the aid of a music cassette, play party games such as musical bumps, musical statues and musical mats. Intersperse the musical games with 'Grandma's footsteps', 'What's the time, Mr Wolf?' or 'Blind man's buff'.

Music

Listen to *Fun with Music: Beethoven's Birthday Party* and *Chou-Chou's Birthday Music* (EMI), also *Children's Party Games* (1988, Playtime tapes).

Useful references

Stories

The Surprise Party P. Hutchins (1972, Picture Puffin)
Alfie Gives a Hand S. Hughes (1985, Armada)
The Jolly Postman A. and J. Ahlberg (1986, Heinemann)
Happy Birthday, Moon F. Asch (1985, Corgi)
Mr Rabbit and the Lovely Present C. Zolotow (1968, Bodley Head)

Homes

What you need

House-shaped plain paper, pencils, coloured pencils, property magazine or house advertisements, adhesive, scissors, plain paper; board and chalk or large sheet of plain paper and thick felt-tipped pen; rulers; toy bricks or cubes, centimetre rulers; large sheet of sugar paper, old catalogue; pictures of religious buildings; photocopiable page 120; example of the window picture, sugar paper or wallpaper scraps, material, stapler; old cardboard boxes.

English
My house

Give each child a sheet of plain A4 paper cut into a simple house shape. Ask the children to fold the paper in half, and divide one side into rooms to show the inside of the house. Ask them to draw furniture and furnishings in these rooms and label each item. Then ask them to write a description of their house on the blank half of the paper (see Figure 1). They could draw the outside of the house on the reverse. Alternatively, you could ask the children to draw and write about an imaginary house or write about a house in a property magazine or house advertisement.

My house

My house has 3 bedrooms and a bathroom upstairs. It has a kitchen, dining room and lounge downstairs.

Figure 1

Lists of items

Children of this age often enjoy making lists. Ask them to choose one of the following rooms and make an inventory: bedroom, lounge, kitchen, bathroom or dining room. Suggest they use some picture dictionaries to help them, if available. Write their lists on the board.

Maths
Ordering the street

Show the children how houses are usually ordered along roads (see Figure 2). Show them how to draw their own road with rulers along a landscape piece of A4 paper with small rectangles numbered on either side to represent houses.

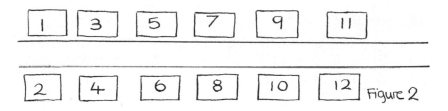

Figure 2

Building a wall

Ask the children to build a wall or tower with toy bricks or cubes. Tell them to measure the width and height of its walls with centimetre rulers.

Science
Electricity in the home

Discuss the uses of electricity in the home. Prepare a large sheet of sugar paper with the heading: 'Household objects that need electricity'. Ask the children to cut out pictures of electrical objects from an old catalogue and stick them on to the sheet.

Making a light

Explain to the class how a simple light can be made (see Figure 3). Provide a few batteries and bulbs and let a small group experiment. Ideally, the bulb and battery voltages should be the same. However, a 3.5V bulb with a 4.5V battery will give a bright light, while a higher voltage bulb will give a dimmer light but last longer. Electricity experiments should always have close adult supervision.

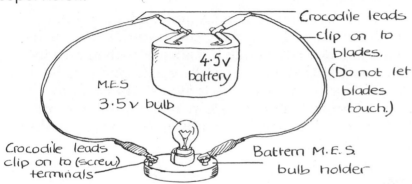

Figure 3

RE

Discuss and, if possible, show pictures of the different kinds of buildings that various faiths worship in, such as churches, synagogues, mosques and temples.

History

Tell the class about the kinds of homes people lived in long ago. Give each child a copy of photocopiable page 120. Ask the children to write a sentence next to each of the pictures.

Geography

Find out if any of the children have been abroad. Ask them if they can remember seeing any houses that were different from the ones in this country. You could point out the countries on a globe and pictures from books of homes in other countries.

Art and craft

Figure 4

Ask the children to draw and colour in pictures of one room in a house, as if they were looking in at a window. Then show them how to cut strips of sugar paper or wallpaper to make a frame for their windows. If there is material available, they could make 'curtains' by stapling rectangles of fabric on either side of their windows (see Figure 4).

Technology

Give the children an assortment of old cardboard boxes, card, paper and adhesives. Ask them to make their own design for a home or just one room.

Music
Songs
'The wise man and the foolish man' in *Okki-tokki-unga*
'When Father papered the parlour' in *Apusskidu*

Useful references
Stories
Moving Molly S. Hughes (1992, J. MacRae)
A House is a House for Me M. A. Hoberman (1982, Picture Puffin)
This is the House that Jack Built P. Adams (1977, Child's Play)
Three Little Pigs (1983, Award Publications)

Minibeasts

What you need

Plain paper, pencils, coloured pencils; board and chalk, rulers, books on minibeasts; plastic or cardboard shapes, scissors, adhesive, large sheets of sugar paper; cardboard ladybird shapes, counters; photocopiable page 121, *The Bad-Tempered Ladybird* Eric Carle (1982, Picture Puffin); bug-boxes or small containers, magnifying lenses; pictures of exotic minibeasts, globe or world map; old egg boxes, blue A5 sugar paper, grey or black wool, adhesive tape, cotton thread; clay or Plasticine or playdough; cardboard boxes, flower catalogues.

English
Minibeast story

Ask the children to imagine they are a minibeast and write a story about what might happen to them, remembering that they are only a few centimetres tall.

Miniwords

Explain that 'mini' means 'little'. Suggest that they write down all the two and three letter words they know how to spell.

Maths
Tessellating shapes

Explain that bees and wasps choose hexagons for the cells that make up their nests. Tell the children that 'tessellate' means fit together. Ask them to draw round plastic or cardboard shapes and discover which ones tessellate. They could cut them out and stick them on to large sheets of sugar paper labelled 'Shapes which tessellate' and 'Shapes which do not tessellate'.

Ladybird sums

Draw a simple ladybird shape on the board (see Figure 1) and show the children how to make up simple sums by counting the ladybird's spots. Ask them to make up their own ladybird sums.

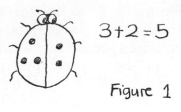

Figure 1

Alternatively, make some simple ladybird shapes (diameter about 12cm) from cardboard. Draw the head and a line down the back but no spots. Then give the children 10 counters (more for Year 2) and ask them to divide their counters on the ladybird's back. Show them how to record their answers to make addition sums. Suggest that they see how many sums they can make from 10 counters.

Time sheet

Read the story of *The Bad-Tempered Ladybird* by Eric Carle. Then give each child photocopiable page 121. Ask them to draw times on each clock beginning with the early morning and working their way through the day. Ask them to write the time underneath each clock and draw a small picture to show to where they think the ladybird might have flown.

Science

If possible, take the children out into the school grounds and ask them to collect one minibeast each in a small container. When they return to the classroom, ask them to look at their creatures with magnifying glasses and draw them carefully. They could either label their drawing or write a description. On completion, they should return the minibeasts to where they found them.

History

Read or tell the story of Robert the Bruce and the spider.

Geography

Tell the children about some of the more exotic butterflies and dangerous minibeasts that live in the tropics and point out the countries where they are found on a globe or a map of the world.

Art and craft

Cut up some old egg boxes into single sections. Demonstrate to the children how to draw a web with chalk on to blue A5 sugar paper. Then make a spider: stick eight short pieces of grey wool to a single egg box section and then draw a face on the spider. Finally, attach the spider to its web with cotton thread (see Figure 2).

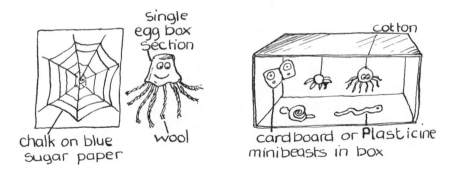

Figure 2

Figure 3

Technology

Ask some children to make a 'minibeast garden' in a cardboard box. Measure and cut paper to fit into the back and the sides of the box. Decorate this either with the children's drawings or by sticking on pictures of flowers from old catalogues. Ask them to make their own minibeasts from cardboard or Plasticine and hang or stick them on to the box (see Figure 3).

PE and drama

Encourage the children to pretend to be minibeasts. Suggest that they: act out the life cycle of a butterfly; make the shapes of various minibeasts (such as worms, beetles, crane flies and snails) or try moving like these creatures (including jumping grasshoppers and buzzing bees). Play 'Follow my leader' as marching ants, and then try 'spider and fly' creeping and pouncing activities.

Music

Listen to *The Flight of the Bumble Bee* (Rimsky-Korsakov) and *Overture to the Wasps* (Vaughan Williams) both on *Fun with Music: Mandy and the Magic Butterfly* (EMI).

Songs

'The ants go marching' in *Okki-tokki-unga*
'I love God's tiny creatures' in *Someone's singing, Lord*
'Eeny meeny minibeasts' and 'Eighteen spiders' in *Scholastic Collections: Songs*
'Inchworm' in *Birds and Beasts: Animal songs, games and activities* S. Roberts (ed.) (1987, A&C Black)

Useful references
Information books
Into Science: *Insects* T. Jennings (1990, OUP)

Stories
The Giant Jam Sandwich J. V. Lord (1988, Piper Picture Books)
The Very Hungry Caterpillar E. Carle (1974, Picture Puffin)
The Very Busy Spider E. Carle (1988, Hamish Hamilton)
The Bad-Tempered Ladybird E. Carle (1982, Picture Puffin)

Myself

What you need

Plain paper, pencils, board and chalk; prepared chart on a large sheet of paper, small pieces of plain paper, coloured pencils or crayons; centimetre rulers, centimetre tape measures; photocopiable page 121; world map, drawing pins; straws, adhesive tape, cardboard circles, wool, adhesive.

English
Hands and feet

Discuss with the class what sort of things they can do with their hands and feet. Ask the children to write the title 'Things I can do with my hand' and then draw round one hand underneath. Tell them to write their ideas inside the outline. Then suggest they do the same with their feet on another sheet of paper titled 'Things I can do with my foot' (see Figure 1).

Figure 1

All about me

Ask the children to write as much as they can about themselves. Tell them that their descriptions will be read out for every one in the class to guess who has written them. Write some guidelines for them on the board such as: 'I am . . . years old. My hair is . . . My eyes are . . . I like . . .'.

Maths
Eye colour chart

If possible before the lesson, prepare a chart as in Figure 2. Ask each child to draw and colour in their eyes on a small piece of paper. Stick these in the appropriate place on the chart. When the chart is complete, discuss the findings with the class. If you do not have time to prepare such a chart, draw four large circles on a large sheet of paper, label each one an eye colour and stick the paper eyes in these circles. A similar chart could be made for hair colour.

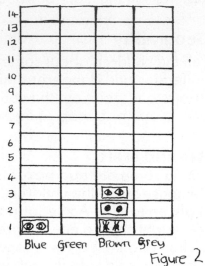

Figure 2

Times in my day

Give each child a copy of photocopiable page 121 with the clocks labelled in order as: 'I wake up', 'Breakfast', 'School starts', 'Playtime', 'Dinner time', 'School finishes', 'Teatime' and 'Bedtime'.

Ask the children to draw the appropriate times on their clocks and record the time underneath. Children who find this difficult can draw the times they know, limiting this to o'clocks.

Measuring with spans

Explain what a 'span' is and show the children how to measure with their spans. Then ask them to draw some large classroom objects (such as a table, chair, cupboard or the board) and record the length and width of these objects using spans.

Science

Ask the children to point to specific parts of their bodies. Discuss with them what the essential requirements are for life. Explain about the bones in our bodies. Then ask the children to draw a straight finger and then one which is bent, labelling the knuckles.

RE

Ask the children if any of them worship regularly. Encourage the children to talk about their individual experiences. Talk about the different faiths in the world and the different ways of worshipping.

Geography

Ask the children if they have visited other countries and point these out on a world map. The children concerned could write their name on a piece of paper which could be pinned on to the map. Ask the children about places they have heard of and would like to visit. If no one has been abroad, use a map of Britain and do likewise.

Art and craft

Happy and sad faces

Prepare some circles of card (about 10cm in diameter). Ask the children to draw and colour in a happy face on one side and a sad face on the other. Wool could be stuck on for hair. Attach a straw to the bottom of the face so the child can twist it round to see the happy or sad face (see Figure 3).

Figure 3

Hand pictures

Ask the children to draw around one or both hands and see what they can turn the shape into.

Music

Experiment with different noises that can be made with our voices and hands.

Songs

'Heads, shoulders, knees and toes', 'Join in the game', 'Everybody do this', 'Do your ears hang low?', 'Put your finger on your head' and 'One finger, one thumb, keep moving' in *Okki-tokki-unga*
'If you're happy' in *Apusskidu*
'Stand up, clap hands, shout thank you, Lord' and 'Hands to work and feet to run' in *Someone's singing, Lord*
'At the ripe old age of one' in *Scholastic Collections: Songs*

Useful references

Stories

Nancy No-Size M. Hoffman (1990, Methuen/Little Mammoth)
Funny-bones A. and J. Ahlberg (1980, Heinemann)
Tall Inside J. Richardson/A. Englander (1989, Picture Puffin)

Poems

'I didn't mean to', 'I was just' and 'I don't want to shrink' in *The Usborne Book of Funny Poems* H. Amery (ed.) (1990, Usborne)

Patterns

What you need

Board and coloured chalks, plain paper, writing pencils, coloured pencils; children's dictionaries; 2cm squared paper, 1cm squared paper, rulers; calculators; computer drawing program; kaleidoscope, mirrors, adhesive tape, short pencil, counters or coins; picture of a mosaic, coloured sticky paper or paper cut from magazines, adhesive; maps; black and coloured thick crayons; greaseproof paper, rulers, black felt-tipped pens; LEGO bricks, cotton reels, art straws, thick paint, sugar paper.

English

Word patterns

Write these three words, spread out in a line, on the board: 'mat', 'ten' and 'hop'. Ask the class to think of words that rhyme with 'mat' and write some of them underneath that word. Ask them to think of rhyming words for themselves and make their own lists. Introduce the children to 'palindromes' (symmetrical words which read the same both ways, such as: 'tot', 'mum' and 'madam'). Suggest that the children find some more examples of palindromes by looking in children's dictionaries.

Writing patterns

Do some simple writing patterns on the board for the children to copy (see Figure 1). They could experiment with different writing materials for each pattern.

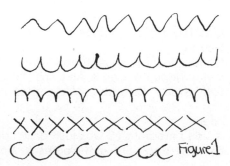

Figure 1

Maths

Making patterns with five squares

On 2cm squared paper show the children different ways of linking five squares together, when one side of each square is adjacent to another. Explain that touching by corners is not acceptable (see Figure 2). Then ask the children to make their own patterns on 1cm squared paper.

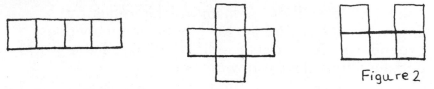

Figure 2

Odd and even number patterns

Ask the children to write the numbers 1 to 20 in order on 2cm squared paper, writing each number in a separate square. Tell them to count in twos and with a coloured pencil ring each even number and then record these numbers underneath. With a different coloured pencil ask them to do the same for the odd numbers.

Using calculators

Demonstrate how to get number multiplication patterns by pressing key 2 on the calculator, then + and then =. Continue pressing the = and see if the children recognise the number pattern appearing. They could record these numbers on paper. Suggest they try the same operation for 5 and 3.

Computers

Suggest to a child using the computer, that he or she tries to make patterns using a drawing program. Encourage the child to experiment with shapes, repetitions, enlargements, colour changes and reversals, depending on the capability of the program.

Science

If possible, let the children look through a kaleidoscope and explain how the patterns are made with mirrors. Join two mirrors together with sticky tape to form a hinge. Stand the mirrors on a flat surface and then ask the children to put a short pencil between them; then a few counters or coins; and then some 1cm squared paper which has been previously coloured in. Suggest to the children that they experiment with moving the mirrors closer together, then further apart (see Figure 3). Can any of the children write their names while looking in a mirror?

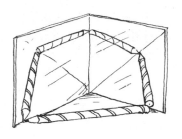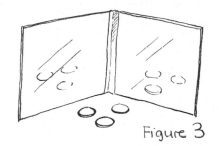

Figure 3

History

Explain that the Romans chose to decorate their houses with mosaics and show pictures, if available. Show the children how to make their own mosaic patterns by using torn or cut small pieces of coloured sticky paper (or coloured paper cut from magazines which would have to be glued into place). Suggest that they arrange the pieces first before sticking them down.

Geography

Get the children to look at some simple maps. Ask them if they can recognise certain key markings such as roads, rivers, the sea and churches.

Art and craft
Patterned windows

Ask the children to cut out a window shape such as an arch, circle, diamond or rectangle from greaseproof paper. Then show them how to draw a continuous scribble line or lines criss-crossing their shape using a ruler and black felt-tipped pen. Finally, get them to colour in the sections with thick crayons to make a patterned window. Challenge the children not to have the same colours side by side. Display the patterns on the classroom window.

Printing

Use classroom items such as LEGO bricks, cotton reels, cubes and art straws for printing, dipping these into thick paint and then on to sugar paper. Encourage the children to experiment with different patterns.

Music

Make sound patterns with the class by clapping, finger clicking and knee slapping and see if the children can copy your rhythms.

Songs

'Oh, we can play on the big bass drum', 'The music man' and 'Johnny taps with one hammer' in *Okki-tokki-unga*

Useful references
Stories

The Willow Pattern Story A. Drummond (1992, North–South Books/ Ragged Bear Books)
The Patchwork Quilt V. Flournoy (1985, Bodley Head)
Elmer: The story of a patchwork elephant D. McKee (1990, Red Fox)

Information books

The Mathematical Patterns File A. Wiltshire (1988, Tarquin)

Roads

What you need

Plain paper, rulers, pencils; pictures of vehicles; board and chalk; travel brochures or old car magazines, scissors, adhesive; photocopiable page 122; pictures of old vehicles; local map; globe; large circles and triangles of white paper, a highway code book, thick felt-tipped pens or paints; card, scissors, paper fasteners; grey sugar paper, adhesive tape.

English
Lists

Write the following categories on the board: 'Cars', 'Big vehicles', 'Slow-moving vehicles' and 'Two-wheeled vehicles'. Set the work out in columns on the board. Then ask the children to make lists under the appropriate headings. You may use only two categories with Year 1. Encourage the children to use books about transport to help them.

Descriptive writing

Ask the children to cut out a picture of a car from a travel brochure (the car hire section is a good source) or magazine and stick this on a piece of plain paper. Ask them to write a description of the car; for example, its colour, number of doors and wheels and the number of people it could carry. You could introduce words such as hatchback, saloon and estate.

Maths

On the board record the number of children who walk, come by car or taxi, bike or bus to school. Give each child a copy of photocopiable page 122 and ask them to fill it in.

Science

Talk to the class about the energy sources used for machines (such as pedal power, batteries, petrol and diesel).

History
Roman roads

Explain that when the Romans occupied Britain they had an extensive road building plan and they always tried to make their roads straight. Refer to any local Roman roads if possible.

History of transport

Show the class some pictures or photographs of old vehicles and talk about these. The children could draw a picture of the one they find the most interesting.

Geography

Show the children a map and explain the different road categories. If possible, have a detailed local map and let the children look at this individually and work out their journey to school. Ask the children to draw the road they live on and their house with its number. Then get them to draw their neighbours' houses and, if possible, number them.

Different types of transport

Show pictures of different forms of transport in other countries. Look at where these countries are on a globe.

Art and craft
Road signs

Prepare some large circles and triangles of white paper. Show the children the road signs in a highway code book. Ask them to choose a sign and copy this on a paper circle or triangle. Alternatively, ask them to make up their own sign.

Moving 2D vehicles

Ask the children to draw a vehicle shape, without the wheels, on card and cut this out. (Alternatively, have a few simple templates for the children to draw round.) Then ask them to fill in the details of the doors and windows on both sides of the card and colour in their vehicles. Next ask them to draw around circle shapes on card and cut these out (or have some ready prepared). Show the children how to attach the wheels to the vehicle with a paper fastener (see Figure 1).

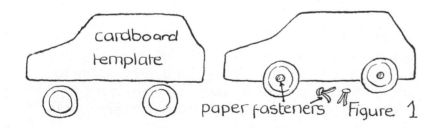

cardboard template

paper fasteners   Figure 1

Roads

Ask the children to make a set of interconnecting roads cut from grey sugar paper. Get them to include features like zebra crossings, roundabouts and road markings. Stick their roads together with adhesive tape. Then ask them to cut pictures of road vehicles from travel brochures or magazines and mount these on to cardboard and add a cardboard stand.

Technology

Ask the children to design a traffic light or Pelican crossing light with cardboard, so that the 'lights' change. Suggest that they could use sliding cards or flaps (see Figure 2).

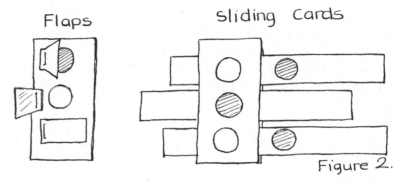

Flaps   Sliding cards

Figure 2.

Music
Songs

'The wheels on the bus' in *Okki-tokki-unga*
'The Fireman' and 'Daisy Bell' in *Apusskidu*
'Motor car' and 'Traffic song' in *Scholastic Collections: Songs*

Useful references
Information books

Fun with Simple Science: Machines and movement B. Taylor (1990, Kingfisher)
Highway Code DoT (1987, HMSO)

Stories

Gumdrop For Ever! V. Biro (1991, Picture Puffin)
Mr Gumpy's Motor Car J. Burningham (1973, Cape)
Meg's Car H. Nicoll/J. Pienkowski (1975, Heinemann)
The Drive H. Oxenbury (1983, Walker)
Topsy and Tim Ride Their Bicycles J. and G. Adamson (1992, Blackie/Penguin)

Trees

What you need

Board and chalk or large sheets of paper and thick felt-tipped pen, plain paper, pencils; cardboard cover, treasury tags and hole punch or stapler; centimetre rulers; 1cm squared paper, coloured pencils; large sheet of sugar paper, adhesive, home catalogue; scissors; globe or map of the world; thickly-mixed powder paint, saucers, brushes, sugar paper; adhesive tape, Blu-Tack, crayons; old card, kitchen foil; wood and woodworking tools; wooden percussion instruments.

English
Words about trees

Talk to the class about words associated with trees. Draw a vertical line with simple leaf shapes on either side of the line and write some tree words in the leaf shapes (see Figure 1). Ask the children to draw their own tree shape and write any other tree words they can think of in the leaf shapes.

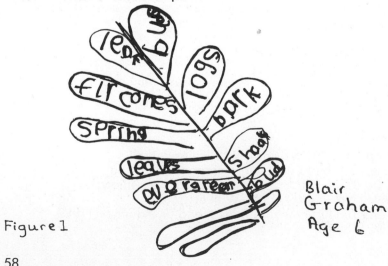

Figure 1

58

My favourite tree book

Talk to the class about different kinds of trees, such as fruit trees, nut-bearing trees, ornamental trees and trees that are good for climbing or in which to build a house. Then ask each child to draw the tree they would like in their garden or near their home, and write why they have chosen that tree. They could cut the paper into the shape of a tree. The children's work could be made into a book later.

Maths
Measuring leaves

Collect a selection of leaves. Ask the children to each draw round a leaf and show them how to measure with a centimetre ruler the width and length of their leaf. Have a sample of how you want them to record their answers, for example: 'My leaf is . . . cm long and . . . cm wide'.

Area of a leaf

Ask the children to place the leaf of their choice on to 1cm squared paper and draw round it. Tell them to colour in the squares in the leaf outline in a variety of colours and then count and record how many whole squares the leaf covered.

Science
Things made from wood

Ask the children to look around the classroom and either draw or write down the things that are made from wood. They could also cut out pictures of objects made from wood from catalogues and stick these on to a large sheet of sugar paper.

Deciduous and evergreen trees

Have a class discussion on the difference between the two types of trees. If possible, show examples of both types of leaves. Ask the children if they know the names of any trees and into which category they fall.

Geography

Tell the children about the kind of trees that grow in a rainforest. Explain simply why it is important to preserve them and show the children on a globe where the rainforests are located.

Art and craft

Leaf prints

Mix up some powder paint in autumnal colours to a thick consistency in saucers. Then ask the children to paint the veined side of the leaves and then press them on to a sheet of sugar paper. They could use the same leaf several times with different colours or print with other leaves.

Leaf foils

Prepare some rectangular pieces of old card cut a little larger than the leaves and some rectangles of kitchen foil paper cut a few centimetres larger than the card. Ask the children to fasten their chosen leaf on to a card with a little Blu-Tack or Plasticine with the veins uppermost. Then get them to place the foil over the leaf and firmly smooth it down until there is a good impression of the leaf showing. The foil can be stuck on the reverse of the card (see Figure 2).

This leaf is stuck on card veins uppermost

Tin foil is spread over and pressed down

Figure 2

Technology

If you have assistance and woodworking materials are available, this would be an ideal opportunity to let the children experiment with wood and some of the tools.

Music

Listen to part of *Peter and the Wolf* (Prokofiev).

Show the class some percussion instruments made from wood and let them experiment with the sounds these instruments make. The instruments could be used to accompany songs about trees.

Songs

'The magic tree' in *Scholastic Collections: Songs*
'Oh, Christmas tree' in *The Nursery Rhyme Book*
''Neath the spreading chestnut tree' in *Okki-tokki-unga*
'Who's that sitting in the sycamore tree?' in *Someone's singing, Lord*

Useful references

Information books
Threads: Wood T. Jennings (1991, A&C Black)
Usborne First Nature: Trees R. Thomson (1980, Usborne)
A Brief Guide To Britain's Principal Trees (free) Forestry Commission

Stories
Where the Forest Meets the Sea J. Baker (1989, Walker)
When Dad Cuts Down the Chestnut Tree P. Ayres (1988, Walker)
The Silver Christmas Tree P. Hutchins (1974, Bodley Head)
The Hurricane Tree L. Purves (1988, Bodley Head)

Instant themes

Weather

What you need
Plain paper, writing pencils, dictionaries and word books (optional); clothing catalogues from classroom, adhesive, scissors, large sheets of paper; photocopiable page 121; prism; photocopiable page 120; world map; sugar paper, art straws, string; card circles, yellow crayon; paper fasteners or drawing pins, 'junk' modelling materials; percussion instruments.

English
Making longer words
Ask the children to choose a weather word and then find as many words as possible which begin with that word (for example sun, sunshine, sunlight, sunbeam and Sunday). They could use simple dictionaries or word books to help them.

Clothes for weather conditions
If there are clothing catalogues in the room, the children could select a picture, cut this out and stick it on a sheet of paper. Then they could write about what the weather might be like when the person is wearing these clothes.

Alternatively, they could draw a picture of themselves playing outside and then write about their favourite kind of weather and the clothes they would wear.

Maths
Counting raindrops
Ask the children to draw a window with four panes of glass. Ask them to draw the same number of raindrops on each pane. Finally, ask them to count and record the total at the bottom of the page (see Figure 1).

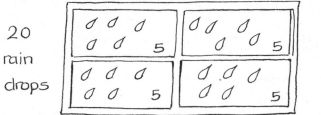

Figure 1

Recording the weather throughout the day
Give each child a copy of photocopiable page 121. This activity will need to be started at the beginning of the day. Ask the children to draw the hands on their clock for the correct time (you might find it simpler to limit this to o'clocks for Year 1) and write the time underneath. Then, alongside each clock, ask them to draw a simple symbol to represent the weather at that time. They can then carry on recording the weather throughout the day.

Science
How rainbows are formed
Explain that we only see rainbows when the sun is behind us and the rain in front. If you can locate a prism (and if the sun is shining), try making a rainbow (see Years 3 and 4 'Colour' theme). Ask the children to colour in a rainbow using the correct colour order (red, orange, yellow, green, blue, indigo, violet). Ask them to add the sun and the rain to their work.

Weather through the seasons

Ask the children to fold a piece of paper into four. Show them on the board (or on a large piece of paper) how they should write the seasons in each section. Then ask them to draw appropriate weather pictures in each section and write what would be the most common seasonal weather.

History

Give each child a copy of photocopiable page 120. Ask them to draw bad weather around the homes. Then ask the children to discuss which of the homes would be well protected and why. They could write one sentence alongside each picture.

Geography

Discuss climates throughout the world. Get the children to draw weather symbols for different parts of the world and pin these to a world map in the appropriate places.

Art and craft

'The sun has got his hat on . . .'

Ask the children to draw round a large circle on to card and cut this out (or have some pre-cut). Show them how to make the sun's rays by cutting into the edge (see Figure 2). They could then decorate their suns with faces using yellow crayon and add a fancy hat made from paper.

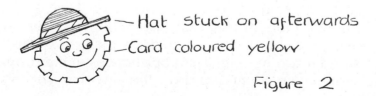

—Hat stuck on afterwards
—Card coloured yellow

Figure 2

Kites

Make an example quickly to demonstrate (see Figure 3). Ask the children to cut a kite shape out of sugar paper. Then they need to cut up some art straws and glue these on the shape. Finally they could attach some string (if available).

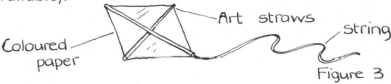

Coloured paper — Art straws — string

Figure 3

Technology

Challenge the children to make a windmill where the sails can turn. They will need junk materials and paper fasteners or drawing pins (or they could use a construction kit).

Music

If you have access to percussion instruments, you could let the children experiment with making sounds to represent different weather.

Songs

'The wise man and the foolish man' in *Okki-tokki-unga*
'Who built the ark?', 'I love the sun' and 'I have seen the golden sunshine' in *Someone's singing, Lord*
'The Weather-or-Nots' in *Scholastic Collections: Songs*
'It's raining, it's pouring' in *The Nursery Rhyme Book*
'Sing a rainbow' in *Apusskidu*
'Sun arise' in *Tinder-box: 66 songs for children*
S. Barratt/S. Hodge (eds.) (1982, A&C Black)

Useful references

Stories

Mrs Mopple's Washing Line A. Hewett (1970, Picture Puffin)
The Wind Blew P. Hutchins (1978, Picture Puffin)
The Amazing Story of Noah's Ark M. Williams (1990, Walker Books)

School

What you need
Board and chalk, plain paper, pencils; photocopiable page 121; rulers, 1cm squared paper (optional); coloured pencils or crayons; black sugar paper; 'junk' modelling materials; school's tape recorder and assembly tapes.

English
People in our school
Ask the children for the names of people who work or help at the school. List these people, on the board, under 'Teachers', 'Helpers', 'Kitchen staff' and 'Office staff'. Ask the children to copy the list (some Year 1 children may find this difficult) and then write: 'I like to talk to . . .'. The children could then fill this in and draw a picture of themselves with one or more adults.

Likes and dislikes at school
Ask the children to fold a piece of plain paper in half. Write on the board: 'Things I like at school' and 'Things I do not like'. Discuss the children's likes and dislikes at school and write down some of the more popular and unpopular activities. Then ask the children to copy the titles and list their favourite and least favourite activities in the appropriate places. (Following on from this, you could let the children choose to do one of their favourite activities, if it is possible.)

Maths
Times at school
Give each child a copy of photocopiable page 121. Work out with the class eight important times at school (such as the beginning of school, assembly, playtime and so on). Write these on the board, with the appropriate times. Ask the children to copy these times, one underneath each clock, and then ask them to mark the correct times on their clocks. Some Year 1 children will need help with this, and may feel happier doing a 'Times in my day' sheet instead (see Years 1 and 2 'Myself' theme).

Classroom plan
Ask the children to imagine that they are looking down on the classroom from the ceiling. Then ask them to draw a plan of the furniture in their classroom, preferably on 1cm squared paper (demonstrate on the board). This could well prove too difficult for Year 1 children, so ask them to draw a rectangle to represent their table and draw circles to represent the children on their table and name these (see Figure 1).

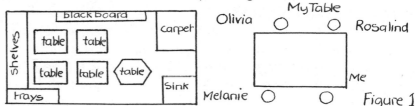

Figure 1

Science
Ask the class to consider what items in the classroom use electricity and where this comes from. Discuss the potential dangers of electricity, particularly sockets and pylons. The children could then draw pictures of the lights and any other electrical appliances in the room. They could also count and draw the electrical sockets in the room.

RE

Have a class discussion about the children's favourite assemblies. Working in small groups, let the children make up short plays about school. Encourage them to include some aspect of helping each other. Some ideas to work on could be: 'The new child', 'A lost book', 'The bully' and 'An accident in the playground'. Let the children watch each other's plays.

History

Explain that children at school in Victorian times used to have slates and slate pencils or chalks with which to do all their work. Then give the children some black sugar paper and chalk and ask them to write out the alphabet. You could even ask them to imagine they are in a Victorian class and have them all sitting individually, facing the board and give a 'formal' handwriting lesson or demonstrate how the alphabet and tables would have been taught by rote.

Geography

Encourage some of the children to describe verbally their journey from their houses to the school. If possible, start with the child who lives closest. Then ask the children to draw a simple outline of the school with the closest road or footpath. Tell them to draw an arrow to show the direction they have to come from. Some children might be able to put more roads or details on their 'maps'.

Art and craft
Drawing the school from the outside

If the weather is fine, take the children outside to do pencil sketches of part of the school building.

Rubbings around the room

Demonstrate how to make a rubbing using plain paper and a crayon. Then ask the children to try rubbing over different objects in the classroom. They should then cut out each rubbing and stick this on to a large sheet of sugar paper and label it.

Technology

Ask the children to make an item of classroom furniture from junk modelling material.

Music

Listen to the children's favourite assembly music and ask for their thoughts on this.

Useful references
Stories
Topsy and Tim Go To School J. and G. Adamson (1988, Penguin)
The Day the Teacher Went Bananas J. Howe/L. Hoban (1987, Picture Puffin)
Dinner Ladies Don't Count B. Ashley (1984, Picture Puffin)

Toys

What you need

Photocopiable page 116 (some with extra words on or only a few pictures), writing pencils, coloured pencils; toy coins; dominoes or card, rulers, scissors; paper strips; plain paper; a few copies of photocopiable page 120; world map; finished example of 'Jack-in-the-box', card, adhesive, paper clips; catalogues or magazines, art straws.

English
Using photocopiable page 116

Photocopy one sheet of photocopiable page 116 and print either the initial letters of the toys or the words themselves (depending on the ability of the children) at the top of the page, then photocopy the number you require.

Ask the children to write the initial letter of each word, or the word itself, alongside the picture. Alternatively, photocopy one sheet, then stick a strip of paper over the second and fourth columns and photocopy the number you require. Then ask the children to write a sentence or two about each toy.

Toys for my friends

Ask the children to write down their friends' names and think of a toy that begins with the same initial letter as their first name (for example 'A ball for Ben' or 'A rabbit for Rosslyn').

Maths
Toy shop

Collect some classroom toys (including books and games) on to a table and label each with a price (up to 20p). Ask a small group to go to the 'shop', select what they want and pay for it with pretend money. They could record what they have bought in pictures and writing, together with the prices and the total they have spent (show them how to set this out on the board). The children could take it in turns to be shopkeepers.

Domino sums

If you cannot locate any dominoes, a group of children could make these from card. Let them do domino sums with **the** dominoes (see Figure 1). They could also play a game in a group where, to begin with, the dominoes are divided evenly. One domino is placed in the centre and then each child in turn has to make the total six by adding a domino either side (see Figure 2). The first child to get rid of his or her dominoes is the winner.

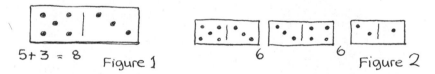

5 + 3 = 8   Figure 1   6   6   Figure 2

Science

Prepare some strips of paper (about 3×15cm) with a slit cut 5cm down from the centre of one end (see Figure 3). Fold one half of the cut part forwards and the other backwards. Hold the 'helicopter' aloft and let it fall. It will twirl around. Let the children work in pairs or small groups. Give them

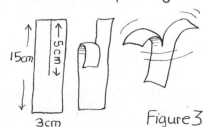

15cm   5cm   3cm   Figure 3

paper and scissors and ask them to experiment with the basic design and see what improvements they can come up with. After a certain time, each group could show the class their findings.

RE

On the board write: 'This is my special toy. (Toy's name) helps me when I . . .'. Then ask the children to copy this and draw a picture of their own special toy and fill in the blanks. You could have a class discussion about why these toys are particularly important to the children and also encourage them to think about how our old toys could help others.

History

Give the children some copies of photocopiable page 120. Discuss what toys children might have made or played with, considering the technology available, at each period. Then tell the children to choose just one picture, cut this out and stick it on a plain piece of paper. Then they should add the toys they think the children at that time would have had.

Geography

Ask the children if any of them have toys from another country. If so, they could draw pictures of the toys and pin their pictures on to the appropriate country on a world map. Check where the toys in the classroom come from and do likewise.

Art and craft
Jack-in-the-box

Have a finished example of this and prepare paper rectangles and strips for the children. Cut out a rectangle of sugar paper or card (about A6 size). Draw the head, chest and arms of a Jack-in-the-box on

another piece of card and cut this out. Cut out a strip of paper (about 15 × 3cm) and fan fold this. Finally, glue one end of the strip on to the 'box' and the other on to the 'Jack' (see Figure 4). The 'Jack' will need to be kept in place with a paper clip.

Figure 4

Stick puppet

If you can find any catalogues or magazines in the classroom, ask the children to cut out a picture of a person or animal and paste this on to card. Then cut the figure out of the card (leaving a border if the children find this more aesthetically pleasing). Finally, fasten a straw on to the card with a piece of adhesive tape.

Music
Songs

'Oh, we can play on the big base drum' and 'Miss Polly' in *Okki-tokki-unga*
'Bananas in pyjamas' in *Apusskidu*

Useful references
Information books

What's inside? Toys S. Bell/A. Parsons (eds.) (1991, Darling Kindersley)

Stories

My Naughty Little Sister and Bad Harry's Rabbit D. Edwards (1990, Methuen Children's Books)
Dogger S. Hughes (1977, Bodley Head)
Paddington Concept Books M. Bond (1990, Collins)
Teddybear Books (series) S. Gretz (1986–, Armada)
Winnie the Pooh A. A. Milne (1991, Little Mammoth)

Years 3 and 4

Space

What you need

White A5 cards, board and chalk, writing pencils, coloured pencils; circular board protractor, rulers, circular protractors; straws, string, adhesive tape, long balloons, calculators; circular pieces of plain paper, globe; white or yellow card, scissors, cotton, rulers, stapler, large sheet of black sugar paper; percussion instruments.

English
Postcard from a planet

Give each child a piece of white A5 card. Ask them to imagine they are on a planet and are sending a postcard to their friends at school on Earth. Get them to draw a picture of their location on one side. Draw a large rectangle on the board to represent the other side. Write the school's address in the right-hand section and in the left-hand section write 'Planet . . .', a date in the future, and 'Dear Class' (see Figure 1). Then tell them to write about the things they have seen and done on the planet.

Figure 1

Thoughts on an alien

Ask the children to imagine a strange alien. They could draw it and then write notes on its particular features (such as its physique, how it moves, communicates and what it eats). Some children may want to turn their ideas into a poem.

Maths
Space aliens

Tell the class to imagine that they have been invaded by a space alien whose diet is a particular number, for example '7'. On the board write a selection of numbers up to 1,000 with number 7 in, for example: 17, 75, 237, 870, 741 and so on. Show the children how the alien 'eats' number 7s, according to their place value, by setting out the following sums on the board: $17-7=10$ $75-70=\square$ $237-7=\square$ $870-70=\square$ $741-700=\square$ Tell the children to copy the sums and fill in the answers. Once the children have the idea they can make up their own sums.

Mathematical star (Year 4 only)

Show the children how to draw a six-pointed star. Draw a circle with a circular board protractor. Mark this off in 60° divisions, write the figures around the circle (e.g. 60°, 120° etc.) and then join the points.

Science
Diameter of the planets

Put the following information on the board: 'Mercury 4,880km; Venus 12,100km; Earth 12,756km; Mars 6,790km; Jupiter 142,800km; Saturn 120,860km; Uranus 52,000km; Neptune 48,400km; Pluto 3,000km'. Ask the children to write down the planets in order from biggest to smallest. Some children will be able to work out the difference in size between the biggest and smallest planets, and the difference between the Earth and Jupiter and Pluto. They could check their answers on a calculator.

Rocket balloon
Thread a straw on to a piece of string long enough to stretch across the classroom. Tie the string across the room a few feet from the floor. Have two pieces of adhesive tape handy. Blow up a long balloon and keep hold of the open end. Attach the balloon to the straw with the tape. Pull the straw and balloon to one end of the string, ensuring that the rounded end of the balloon is facing the far end. Then let go (see Figure 2).

Figure 2

Geography
Ask the children to imagine they are in a rocket looking back on Earth. Ask them to draw their view of the Earth, by studying a globe from one angle. This looks effective when drawn on a plain circular piece of paper.

Art and craft
Ask the children to make two six-pointed stars the same size (see 'Mathematical star') out of white or yellow card. Year 3 could draw round a template. Show them how to draw lines from star point to opposite point and joining the intervening points, so that all the lines cross in the centre (see Figure 3). Score each of these lines, then pinch each star point so the star has a 3D effect. Finally, staple the two stars together and attach some cotton to make a mobile. Alternatively, some children could work together and stick single 3D stars on a large sheet of black sugar paper to form a constellation.

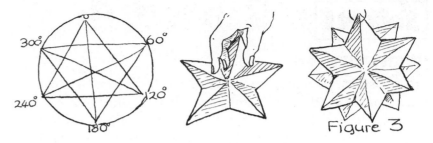

Figure 3

Music
Listen to part of *The Planets* Suite (Holst). Divide the class into four groups, each with a selection of percussion instruments. Set each group the task of making sounds to represent part of a space journey, for example: 'take-off', 'travelling through space', 'a strange planet' and 'aliens'.

Songs
'Battle song of the Zartians' in *Apusskidu*
'Rocket to the stars' and 'Into orbit' in *Scholastic Collections: Songs*

Useful references
Information books
The Usborne Book of Space Facts S. Reid (1987, Usborne)

Stories
Living Fire and other SF stories N. Fisk (1990, Swift)
Dr Xargles Book of Earthlets J. Willis (1988, Andersen Press)
Legends of the Sun and Moon E. and T. Hadley (1983, CUP)
'Many moons' in *Stories for Eight-Year-Olds* S. and S. Corrin (eds.) (1971, Faber)
Extract from *Trillions* (N. Fisk) in *I Like This Story: A taste of 50 favourites* K. Webb (ed.) (1986, Puffin)

Poetry
Spaceways J. Foster (ed.) (1986, OUP)
Rockets and Quasers: Poems for children J. Rice (1984, The Aten Press)

Secrets

What you need

Plain paper, pencils; board and chalk; lemon juice, sticks or nibbed pens, white candles or white wax crayons, cartridge paper, paint, water; detailed local maps; 'hidden object' picture puzzles; cardboard; cotton wool, wool, adhesives, hat elastic; percussion instruments.

English
Secret signs

Talk to the class about signs that people make (such as thumbs-up, a Brownie handshake or touching the side of your nose to indicate you know something). Ask the children to devise some secret signs that mean specific things only to them and to write these down.

Secret club

Ask the children to imagine they are forming a club or group in order to do something helpful in secret. Give suggestions, such as tidying a room, a surprise party or making a special present. Ask them to write about who would be in their group, how they would organise themselves and how they would finally reveal the 'surprise'.

My secret friend

Ask the children to imagine that they have a 'secret' friend and to write a story about him or her. This could be someone who is invisible and only talks to them, or someone who appears to them only at night, or someone they write to or phone and no one knows about. The person could be magical or an alien, but the main point of the story should be the secrecy element.

Maths
Guess my secret number

The children can work in pairs or small groups. One child thinks of a number and writes this down secretly. The other children ask five questions, to which they can only have a 'yes' or 'no' answer in order to guess the secret number.

Alphabet code sums

Write the alphabet on the board with 26 numbers underneath.

A	B	C	D	E	F	G	H	I	J	K	L	M
1	2	3	4	5	6	7	8	9	10	11	12	13
N	O	P	Q	R	S	T	U	V	W	X	Y	Z
14	15	16	17	18	19	20	21	22	23	24	25	26

Ask the children to copy this and then think of a three-letter word (four for Year 4) and write this in secret. Then, ask them to make up a sum for each letter, for example: 'TAP': for T, $10 \times 2 = \Box$;
for A, $199 - 198 = \Box$; for P, $8 \times 2 = \Box$.
When they have finished, the children can exchange their sums and work out the secret words.

Science

Show the children how to write a message in lemon juice with a stick or nibbed pen. When dry, heat this over a radiator to reveal the message. Or show them how to write with a white candle or white wax crayon on to cartridge paper. Brush over with a thin wash of paint to see the writing. Finally, show them how to wet a piece of paper and write a message with a stick. When the paper dries, hold this to the light and the message should appear. Now let the children experiment with their own secret messages.

RE

Explain that throughout history, and even today, some people have had to practise their religion in secret because it is against the laws of their country. For example, tell the children about the Roman persecution of the first Christians.

History

Throughout history, people have had ways of sending secret messages to each other. Tell the class about American Indians sending smoke signals, smugglers using lamps, Africans banging drums and the Enigma code used by the Germans in the Second World War.

Geography

Show the children some highly detailed maps, of the local area if available. Ask the children to imagine that they have hidden a secret message somewhere in the locality and write this place on a piece of paper. Then ask them to write instructions on how to find the message from the school. (You could encourage Year 4 to use grid points and compass directions.) The children can then exchange their instruction notes and work out where the messages are hidden.

Art and craft
Hidden objects

Show the children some 'hidden object' puzzle pictures, found in young children's comics or pre-school books. Ask the children to devise such a picture, preferably a black and white drawing.

Secret card

Explain to the children why some cards are sent secretly. Then ask the children to design a card for someone they know. This could be a Valentine card, a 'Cheer up' or 'Get better soon' card or a 'Thank you' card.

Technology

Ask the children to make disguises for themselves (such as cardboard glasses, false beards and moustaches) using cardboard, paper, cotton wool or coloured knitting wool, adhesives and hat elastic.

Music

Let the children work in pairs with percussion instruments to send messages to each other.

Useful references
Stories

The Secret Garden F. H. Burnett (1985, Armada)
'Secrets' in *Stories Round the World* D. Grant (ed.) (1990, Hodder & Stoughton)

Monsters

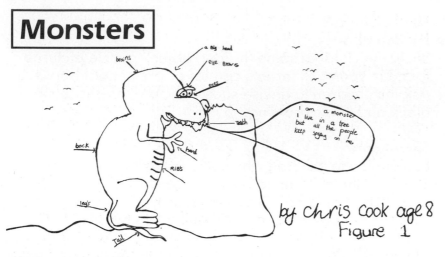

by chris cook age 8
Figure 1

What you need

Dictionaries, pencils, plain A4 paper; plain A3 paper, coloured pencils; metre rulers; photocopiable page 121; calculators, rulers; books on animals and birds, coloured pencils; folktales about giants and dragons; A4 card, crayons, felt-tipped pens, hat elastic or cardboard strips, scissors, adhesive; plain A5 paper; 'junk' materials, adhesives; percussion instruments.

English
Monstrous words

Challenge the children to find words in dictionaries which have more than ten letters. Suggest that they start at the initial letter of their own name. All the words could be compiled on to one class list.

Made-up monster

Ask the children to draw an imaginary monster on to plain A3 paper and label the different features on their monster. Help them to make up a simple two-line rhyming chant and write this in a speech bubble from the monster's mouth (see Figure 1).

Monster story

Ask the children to write a story in which they discover a monster (this could be about their made-up monster) and have an adventure together. Their monster could either be friendly or dangerous.

Maths
Monster numbers

Ask the children to list some mathematical features about their monster. You could put these suggestions on the board:

'My monster's height is . . . m. Its weight is . . . kg. Its waist is . . . cm. It lives for . . . years. It sleeps . . . hours a day.'

Year 4 could compare these measurements with their own measurements.

Monster's day

Give each child a copy of photocopiable page 121 with the 'Monster's day' added to the page. Ask them to imagine what their monster might be doing during the day, put the times on the clock faces and write the activity underneath. Some children could add the time digitally under each clock as well.

Monstrous calculations

Challenge the children to make up sums using numbers in their thousands (hundreds for Year 3). Record these, estimate what the answers will be and then try them on the calculator. Show the children how to set out their work in columns on the board. (They can get a rough estimate by adding the 'hundred' or 'thousand' numbers and ignoring the rest.)

My sum	My estimate	Answer on the calculator
4782 + 6539	12,000	11,321

Science
Ask the children to look through books on animals and birds and see if they can find any pictures of monstrous creatures living today (they could be monstrous in size or appearance). They could then draw their chosen creature and give a short description of its life style.

History
Read or tell stories of giants and dragons from folk tales and explain briefly about the period in which they are set.

Art and craft
Masks
Demonstrate how to make a simple monster mask from A4 card (see Figure 2). Show the children how to help each other to mark on the eye holes. The eye slots can then be cut and the card cut into a monster's face with ears and/or horns. The children can then decorate their monster faces with crayons or felt-tipped pens. Finally, show them how to staple hat elastic or a cardboard strip to the mask so that it can be worn.

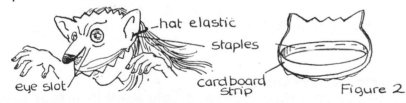

Figure 2

Monster consequences
This is a game for a small group of children. Give each child a sheet of plain A5 paper and get them to draw a monster's head at the top of the paper, without letting the others see. Tell them to fold over the head drawing, leaving just the neck showing, and pass the paper on to another child. Each child then draws on a body and arms and folds this over, leaving the bottom of the 'waist' showing, and passes it on. Finally, each child

draws the legs and feet. The papers are then opened to reveal some amazing monsters.

Technology
Ask a group to design and make a monster from 'junk' materials. The monster should be as large as a child. Suggest that they plan out the monster first and then let each child be responsible for making and attaching a part of the body.

Music
Listen to part of the *Peer Gynt* Suite (Grieg). Divide the children into groups with percussion instruments and encourage them to experiment with sounds and rhythms which represent a monster.

Songs
'The prehistoric animal brigade' and 'After the ball was over' in *Okki-tokki unga*
'Maggon, the bad-tempered dragon' in *Apusskidu*
'Puff the magic dragon' in *Tinder-box: 66 songs for children* S. Barratt/S. Hodge (1982, A&C Black)
'It's a monster . . . Isn't it?' in *Scholastic Collections: Songs*

Useful references
Stories
The BFG R. Dahl (1982, Cape)
'The great white cat' and 'Two giants' in *Stories Round the World* D. Grant (ed.) (1990, Hodder & Stoughton)
Extract from *The Iron Man* in *The Puffin Book of 20th Century Children's Stories* J. Elkin (ed.) (1991, Puffin)
Heroes and Monsters: Greek legends retold J. Reeves (1987, Piccolo)

Poetry
There's an Awful Lot of Weirdos in our Neighbourhood C. McNaughton (1990, Walker)

Lights

What you need

Black A4 sugar paper, pencils, plain paper, adhesive; lined paper, board and chalk; photocopiable page 120; torches, rulers; batteries, battery holders, small bulbs, crocodile clips, card, paper fasteners, foil; photocopiable page 121; globe, yellow ball; empty toilet rolls, gold foil, cotton tape or hat elastic, evergreen leaves, adhesive tape; sugar paper.

English
In the dark

Ask the children to write sentences about how they feel when there is no light. Get them to cut out their sentences and stick them separately on to black sugar paper (see Figure 1).

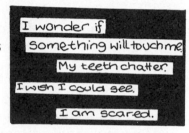

I wonder if
Something will touch me
My teeth chatter.
I wish I could see.
I am scared.

Figure 1

Light web

Write the word 'light' in the centre of the board and put a ring around it. Ask the children for things that they associate with light and write these around the word. Then pick one word, for example 'sun', and ask for more words associated with that and make an extension to the web. The children can then make their own word webs.

Maths
Lighting-up times

Give each child a copy of photocopiable page 121. On the board write the heading 'Lighting-up times' and the following: 'Jan. 5pm, Feb. 6pm, March 7pm, April 8pm, May 9pm, June 10pm, July 9pm, August 8pm, Sept. 7pm, Oct. 6pm, Nov. 5pm and Dec. 4pm'. Check that the class understands the abbreviations and explain that these are approximate lighting-up times in England. (Don't worry about British Summer Time!) Ask the children to choose eight months to record the times on their clocks. Ask older children to think of a day in a month and 'correct' the time by adding on 2 minutes per day for January to June, and subtracting 2 minutes per day for July to December; for example: for 10 April 8.20pm or 5 Nov. 4.50pm.

Measuring the spotlight

Working in pairs, ask one child to hold a torch 5cm above a large piece of paper and another child to draw around the beam of light. Explain what a diameter is. Ask the second child to measure the diameter of the beam and record the answer. Now ask the first child to hold the torch 10cm away and the other child to draw and measure the new circle. They could carry on until they run out of paper. Ask if they can see any connection between the distance of the torch from the paper and the diameter of the beam.

Science
Making a light switch

Show the class how to make a light work (see Year 1 and 2 'Homes' theme 'Making a light'.) Then show them how a simple switch can be made with a small piece of cardboard and foil (see Figure 2).

tin foil

paper fasteners

cardboard

Figure 2 (a)

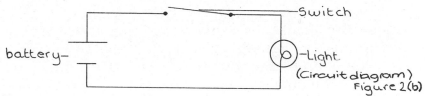

(Circuit diagram)
Figure 2(b)

RE

If possible have some books and magazines about festivals available. Ask the children to choose one festival of light, read about it and then write about it in their own words. They could illustrate their work. Suitable festivals might include Bonfire night, Christingle, Sancta Lucia, the Sikh festival of Diwali, the Chinese Lantern Festival, the Hindu festival of Holi, the Buddhist Festival of Lights and the Jewish festival of Hanukah.

History

Tell the class a brief history of using light. Cave men would have used the moon and firelight. For centuries, ancient civilisations relied on oil-, rush- and tallow-lamps. Candles were used from the Middle Ages to the nineteenth century, when gas-lamps came into use. The first light bulb was made by the American Thomas Edison in 1879. In 1895, a German scientist, Wilhelm Roentgen discovered X-rays and this work was improved by the discovery of radium by Marie Curie in 1898. Give the children photocopiable page 120 and ask them to draw and describe the kinds of light that would have been used in each home.

Geography

Show the children how the Earth turns on its axis every 24 hours, with the aid of a globe and a yellow ball to represent the sun. The children could list all the countries that are in darkness when it is daylight for us.

Art and craft

Help each child to make six white candles (see Reception 'Preparing for Christmas' theme). Fringe the base of these candles so that they will stand upright on a round piece of card. Cover the rest of the card with evergreens (which can be held in place with adhesive tape). Attach some hat elastic or cotton tape to the crown so that it can be secured on to the child's head (see Figure 3).

Figure 3

Music

Listen to *Morning* (Grieg). This is useful for dance work on waking up.

Songs

'Give me oil in my lamp' in *Come and Praise*
D. Coombes (ed.) (1990, BBC)
'Morning has broken' and 'When lamps are lighted in the town' and *Someone's singing, Lord*
'Hanukka candles' in *Scholastic Collections: Songs*

Useful references

Information books and packs
Bright Ideas: Festivals J. Bennett/A. Millar (1988, Scholastic)
Bright Ideas: Easter J. Fitzsimmons (1988, Scholastic)
Weather, Sound and Light (resource pack) (1990, Scholastic)

Stories
'Baba Yaga's daughter' in *Stories Round the World* D. Grant (ed.) (1990, Hodder & Stoughton)

Poetry
Let's Celebrate: Festival poems J. Foster (ed.) (1989, OUP)

Holidays

What you need

Board and chalk, pencils, coloured pencils, passport, plain A4 paper or card; calculator; photocopiable page 121; globe, yellow ball, atlases; pictures of Victorian seaside holidays; tracing paper; A3 paper; clothes catalogues, household catalogues, adhesive; cardboard boxes; folk or traditional music from other countries.

English
Passport

Show the children an example of a passport. Then ask them each to fold a piece of A4 card in half to represent the outside of their passports and fold another piece of paper in half for the inside. Show the children how to make their own passport (see Figure 1). On the front they should write their name and EUROPEAN COMMUNITY (UK) PASSPORT (or a nationality of their choice) and a made-up passport number. Inside on the left page they should fill in details such as 'Place of birth', 'Date of birth', 'Nationality', 'Height' and 'Usual signature'. On the right page they should draw a portrait of themselves. Ask them to pretend they have visited various countries. Write these names in various shapes to represent immigration stamps (see Figure 1).

Figure 1

My holiday

If you have chosen to do this theme at the end of term, you could ask the children to write about what they hope to do during the holidays. If you are doing this during the first week of term, you could ask the children to give a written account of what they did during the holidays.

Maths
Time zones

Give each child a copy of photocopiable page 121 with a time drawn on the first clock and labelled 'Greenwich Mean Time' and then on the other clocks the labels 'Switzerland: 1 hour forward', 'Turkey: 3 hours forward', 'India: 5 hours forward', 'Japan: 9 hours forward', 'Brazil: 3 hours back', 'New York: 5 hours back' and 'Alaska: 11 hours back'. Show the children a globe. Explain that the world is divided into 24 time zones. Ask them to draw the correct times on their sheets. Year 4 children could also write the times digitally underneath.

Currency

Explain that each country has its own currency. Write the following on the board and explain that these are all worth approximately £1.00: 3 (DM) German Deutschmarks, 10 (Fr) French francs, 2 Canadian dollars, 226 Japanese yen, 180 Spanish pesetas and 1.85 ($) American dollars (for Year 4 only). Ask the children to work out how much they would get in each currency for £2.00 and then £10.00. (Year 4 children could choose two other numbers as well.)

Science

Show the class a globe. Ask one child to hold a yellow ball to represent the sun. Show the children how the earth moves on its axis. Then explain how the earth moves around the sun. Show that countries closer to the Equator are hotter. Ask the children to list the hottest and coldest countries in the world.

RE

Explain that many religions affect the way people live their lives. If the children have chosen a certain country for their holiday work, get them to find out about the main religion of that country.

History

Tell the children that people have only been on holiday abroad comparatively recently. If possible, show the children some pictures or old photographs of Victorian seaside holidays.

Geography

Ask the children to draw or trace a map of their chosen holiday destination, marking where they would hope to stay, main towns and places of interest.

Art and craft

Posters

If possible, show the children an example of a holiday poster. Ask them to design a poster on A3 paper and consider the things that would attract people to a particular country.

Designing holiday clothes

Ask the children to draw pictures of themselves in their own 'designer wear' holiday clothes.

Holiday collage

Ask the children to carefully cut some holiday pictures out of travel brochures, clothes and household catalogues. Tell them to lay out their pictures in an interesting way on coloured sugar paper, before sticking them down.

Technology

Challenge the children to draw a design for a suitcase that could double up as something else useful for travelling (such as a seat, trolley, tray or game). Then encourage them to make it using cardboard boxes.

PE and dance

Teach the children some simple folk dances, such as a 'Strip the willow', 'Circassian circle', 'Cumberland square eight' or a simple Greek or Israeli circle dance.

Music

Listen to folk or traditional music from other countries (of the kind that holiday-makers might hear) – for example from *Songs, Games and Stories from Around the World* (cassette and story-book) (UNICEF).

Songs

'Oh island in the sun' and 'I do like to be beside the seaside' in *Ta-ra-ra boom-de-ay*

Useful references

Stories

'The Holiday' in *The Fib and Other Stories* G. Layton (1981, Armada) and in *Funny Stories* M. Rosen (ed.) (1988, Kingfisher)

Friends

What you need

Board and chalk, pencils, plain paper; board compass; calculators; coloured pencils; calligraphy books, computer; 'junk' materials, adhesives; PE apparatus; percussion and tuned instruments.

English
Describe a friend

Ask each child to choose one person in the class (without telling anyone) and to write a description of him or her. Tell them to include physical characteristics, personality and interests and encourage them to say why they like the person. The title could simply be 'My friend' and you could give some guidelines for ideas on the board. When the descriptions are complete, they could be read out to the class for them to try to guess the identity of each person.

Telephone conversation

Ask the children to draw two pictures, one of themselves and another of a friend, each holding a telephone receiver. Then ask them to write a few sentences in speech bubbles imagining that they are having a telephone conversation with their friend. Some children will be able to do two or three speech bubbles for each person, numbering them in order.

Letter to a pen-friend

Explain what a pen-friend is. Show the children how to set out a letter, on the board, using the school's address. Ask the children to write a letter to an imaginary pen-friend about themselves and their school.

Maths
Venn diagrams

Show the children how to make Venn diagrams by drawing two overlapping circles on the board inside a large rectangle. Label the two circles with activities that children might enjoy doing, for example 'swimming' and 'reading' (see Figure 1). Ask the children whether they enjoy these activities and write their names in the appropriate circles. If they enjoy both, then their names go in the central section where the circles overlap. If they enjoy neither, then their names go outside the circles but inside the rectangle. Ask the children to make their own Venn diagrams on plain paper. Some children may like to add a third circle, which overlaps with the other two circles, for a third activity.

Figure 1

Friendly numbers

Ask the children to work out which would be the most useful class size for dividing children up into groups. Suggest the class can be any size between 10 and 40 pupils (or 10 to 20 for children who may find this difficult). Demonstrate with the number 12, showing that it can be divided by 2, 3, 4 and 6. They could use calculators by using the ÷ key.

Science

Discuss how the class could be 'friends to the earth'. Encourage them to think about such issues as litter, pollution and deforestation. They could design a poster with the heading 'Please be a friend to the earth'. Some children might also like to draw and write about caring for animals in the wild or for pets.

RE

Friendship flowers or trees

Make a list of things which make a good friend. Tell the children either to draw a flower with large open petals or a tree with bushy sections (see Figure 2). Ask them to write the things they feel are important in a friend on each petal or leafy section.

Figure 2.

The good Samaritan

Read or tell the story of the good Samaritan (Luke 10: 25–37). The story lends itself to drama work. You could also ask the children to make up a similar story in a modern day setting, for example a road accident where people are in too much of a hurry to care or don't wish to be involved. As a follow-up, you could tell the children about the work of the 'Samaritans'.

Art

Drawing portraits

The children will need to work in pairs. Encourage the model to sit still and the artist to look constantly at their friend as they draw.

Friends' names

Ask the children to find out the full names of some children in the class and then write these out, experimenting using different calligraphy styles and letter sizes. This could be done on the computer, experimenting with different fonts and sizes.

Technology

Ask the children to design and construct a 'classroom friend' from 'junk' and cardboard. For example, this might be a face that smiled, or a waving hand.

PE

The children could work with a friend on a variety of activities, such as working on the apparatus, using balls, mats, 'Follow my leader' activities and chasing games (such as 'Chain tag' and 'Stick-in-the-mud').

Music

A group of children could work together to prepare a musical sequence, using percussion and tuned instruments which could be performed to the class.

Songs

'When I needed a neighbour' in *Someone's singing, Lord*
'F.R.I.E.N.D.S.' in *Scholastic Collections: Songs*

Useful references

Stories

'Baba Yaga's daughter' in *Stories Round the World* D. Grant (ed.) (1990, Hodder & Stoughton)
'The balaclava story' in *The Fib and Other Stories* G. Layton (1981, Armada)
Extracts from *Charlotte's Web* and *Stig of the Dump* in *The Puffin Book of 20th Century Children's Stories* J. Elkin (ed.) (1991, Puffin)

Eggs

What you need

Plain A4 paper, pencils; photocopiable page 119; hard-boiled egg, masking tape or chalk; books on birds and animals; world map; card, crayons, small branch, flower pot filled with earth; example of a chick-in-an-egg, 2cm-wide strips of coloured paper, scissors.

English
Egg words

Ask the children to draw a large egg on plain A4 paper and fill it with words associated with an egg. Alternatively, they could think of words beginning with ex- and change them to begin with egg-, for example: eggtraordinary or eggcellent. Another idea might be to find sayings associated with eggs and write them around the outside, for example: 'Don't put all your eggs in one basket'.

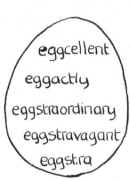

eggcellent

eggactly

eggstraordinary

eggstravagant

eggstra

Story of an egg

Ask the children to imagine that a hard-boiled egg has managed to escape from a saucepan before being eaten and rolls away. Ask the children to write a story about some adventures this egg might have if it were picked up by different people and then rolled off to interesting places.

Maths
Egg box sums

Give each child one copy of photocopiable page 119 with the following written over each box: 'Size 6 42p', 'Size 5 48p', 'Size 4 54p', 'Size 3 60p', 'Size 2 66p' and 'Size 1 72p' and the following written underneath each box: '1 egg costs ☐'. Then ask the children how they would find out how much one egg would cost and fill in the sheet. (You can change the prices but they must be multiples of six.) On the back of the sheet they could make up sums about the eggs, for example Year 3 children could add the different egg-box prices together, while Year 4 could add a few of various sizes of egg together. Alternatively, set some appropriate sums on the board.

Egg rolling competition

Bring in a hard-boiled egg. Stick some masking tape or draw a chalk mark on the floor as a starting point and then ask each child in the class to see how far they can roll the egg. Each child should measure and record the distance and place a chalk mark or strip of thin masking tape where the egg reaches if he or she is in the lead.

Science

Discuss the kinds of creatures that hatch from eggs. You could limit this to hard-shelled eggs or the topic could be broadened to include insects, amphibians, fish and crustaceans. Divide the class into groups and give each a specific category of creatures that lay eggs and ask them to collect as many names of animals in their category as they can.

RE

The symbol of an egg means new life. Discuss this with the children. Eggs are associated with Easter because Christians think of the Resurrection as a renewal of life and egg-rolling is thought to commemorate rolling away the stone from Christ's tomb. If you are doing this theme around Easter, you could read or tell the Easter story.

Geography

Tell the class about egg customs around the world and point out the countries on a map of the world. In Poland and Hungary the eggs are first blown and then covered in beeswax in which a design is scratched. The eggs are then soaked in dye and the wax removed by gently heating the eggs. In Lithuania, large hollow artificial eggs are made and filled with models made from fondant. Children in Germany make nests of moss in the garden hoping that the Easter hare will fill them with eggs.

Art and craft

card egg   oval frames   slits   Figure 1

3D egg mobiles

Cut out an egg shape from a piece of A5 card and colour this in on both sides with a simple crayoned pattern. Cut oval frames of varying sizes from other pieces of A5 card. Cut slits at the top and bottom of the frames and slide them over the 'egg' to make a 3D effect (see Figure 1). These could then be turned into mobiles or hung from a branch stood upright in a flowerpot filled with soil.

Chick-in-an-egg

Have a ready-made model to show (see Figure 2). Have some strips of coloured paper 2cm wide cut to the required lengths (64cm, 30cm, 2 × 20cm, 2 × 10cm, 15cm) or let the children measure for themselves and put the measurements on the board. Take one strip (64cm long), make an egg shape and stick it in place on a base card. Then make three circles for the body, one large (30cm), one medium (20cm) and one small (10cm) and stick the down the circles (see Figure 2). Make one medium head circle (15cm) and one small head circle (10cm). A fringed tail (20cm) and a beak can then be added.

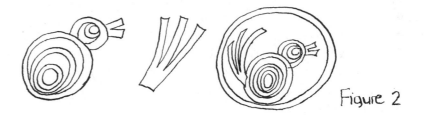

Figure 2

Technology

Suggest that the children attempt to make a 3D hollow egg shape from card.

Useful references

Information books
Bright Ideas: Easter Activities J. Fitzsimmons (1988, Scholastic)

Stories
The Hen Who Wouldn't Give Up J. Tomlinson (1991, Mammoth)
'The nest egg' (P. Pearce) in *Once Upon a Planet* J. Porritt (ed.) (1989, Puffin)

Poetry
A Packet of Poems J. Bennett (ed.) (1986, OUP)
A Picnic of Poetry A. Harvey (ed.) (1990, Puffin)
Egg Poems J. Foster (ed.) (1991, OUP)

Dinosaurs

What you need

Plain paper, pencils; board and chalk, dinosaur reference books; dictionaries; metre rulers, rulers; 2cm squared paper, coloured pencils; fossils, shells, Polyfilla, Vaseline or petroleum jelly, small containers; map of world at time of dinosaurs or modern map of world, drawing or mapping pins, small pieces of paper; pastels, paints, black sugar paper, scissors, adhesive; art straws or white cardboard; crêpe paper, tissue paper, Plasticine or clay, large empty boxes, adhesive tape; 'junk' materials, paper fasteners.

English

Newspaper report

Ask the children to imagine they are a newspaper reporter. Someone tells them they have seen a small dinosaur in their house. They should write a report for the newspaper as if they had spoken to the observer.

Unusual words

Write a list of dinosaurs on the board, such as Iguanodon, Pterosaur, Ichthyosaur, Pteranodon, Hypsilophodon and Tyrannosaur. First get the children to try and pronounce the names. Then ask them to choose a name, record this and find out about the kind of dinosaur it is. Then ask them to find other words which begin with the same three letters as their chosen dinosaur by using a dictionary, recording the words and their meanings. Some children may be able to research more than one word.

Maths
Dinosaur length

Write these facts on the board: Hypsilophodon 2m, Stegosaur 6m, Iguanodon 9m, Tyrannosaur 12m, Brontosaur 21m and Diplodocus 27m. Ask the children to make a list of these dinosaurs and then, using a metre ruler, find or imagine something that would be the equivalent length. The work could be set out as a table:

Dinosaur	About the size of . . .
Hypsilophodon 2m	the board

Comparing dinosaurs

On 2cm squared paper draw a chart to compare the length of dinosaurs (see Figure 1).

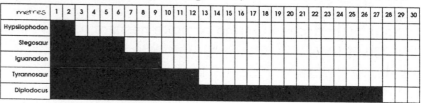

1 square = 1 metre   Figure 1

Science

Show the children some examples of fossils. Explain how they are made. Mix up some Polyfilla to a stiff consistency and pour this into a small shallow container. Tell the children they are going to make some classroom fossils. Grease a shell with petroleum jelly and sink it into the Polyfilla. Leave this until the plaster is dry and then remove the shell. They could then push Plasticine

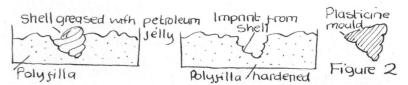

Figure 2

into this 'mould', showing how a solid fossil made from mineral deposits can form (see Figure 2). This work needs to be done in the morning to allow the Polyfilla time to set.

RE
Research different religious accounts of how the world was created.

History
Explain Darwin's theory of the origin of species in very simple terms, up to the dinosaurs. Dinosaurs lived 140 to 147 million years ago. Ask the children to propose theories as to why they were wiped out. Draw a chronological development of animals up to the dinosaur period.

Geography
Show the class a map of the world in the age of the dinosaurs, if available. Alternatively, find out where the dinosaurs lived, draw small pictures of them and pin them on a map of the world.

Art and craft
Silhouette pictures
Ask the children to colour a background of hues of reds and oranges with pastels or paint. Then ask them to cut out a dinosaur shape from black sugar paper, and when the paint is dry, stick this on to the background.

Dinosaur skeletons
Show the children pictures of dinosaur skeletons. Ask them to cut up either art straws or white cardboard to represent the bones and stick these on to black sugar paper in the form of a skeleton.

Prehistoric scene
Working in a group, suggest that the children find a large box and put this on its side. Then cover the inside of the box with red paper with volcanoes painted on it.

They could then try to make dinosaurs and prehistoric ferns, creepers and flowers from Plasticine, clay and crêpe or tissue paper. The outside of the box could be painted or covered with sugar paper (see Figure 3).

Figure 3

Technology
Challenge the children to make a dinosaur head with a moving jaw. This could be in a 2D form using paper fasteners or a 3D model using boxes and hinges.

Music
Listen to 'Fossils' from *The Carnival of the Animals* (Saint-Saëns).

Songs
'Listen to the chorus' in *Okki-tokki-unga*
'When a dinosaur's feeling hungry' in *Tinder-box: 66 songs for children* S. Barratt (ed.) (1982, A&C Black)
'The land that time forgot' and 'The big beasts' boogie' in *Scholastic Collections: Songs*

Useful references
Information books
The Usborne Book of Prehistoric Facts A. Craig (1986, Usborne)
All About Dinosaurs M. Benton/A. Winterbotham (1992, Kingfisher)

Stories
Extract from *Stig of the Dump* in *Puffin Book of 20th Century Children's Stories* J. Elkin (ed.) (1991, Puffin)
Tar Pit T. Seidler (1988, Gollancz)
How the Whale Became and Other Stories T. Hughes (1989, Faber)

Colour

What you need

Board, coloured and white chalk or large sheet of paper and felt-tipped pens, plain paper, pencils, coloured pencils or crayons; circular board protractor, circular protractors, colour wheel, cardboard circles notched at 30°, rulers; computer, art program; glass of water, prism, card, shallow container, water, mirror, Blu-Tack, torch; example of a whirler, white card, hole puncher, string; powder paints, paint-strip cards.

English

Ask the children to choose a colour, think of all the words beginning with that colour and then turn this into a poem. Alternatively, ask them to begin each line of their poem with the name of the colour and then write about it. A further idea is to ask them to think about their feelings associated with the colour.

> Green is a colour, natural and true
> For countryside, meadows and fields too.
>
> Purple's a colour, vain and proud
> Quite a show off, but brings up a crowd.
>
> Cassandra Hillson

Maths
Colour wheel

Show the children a colour wheel (either ready-made or bought, see Figure 1). Show them how to divide a circle into 12 sections by using a circular protractor and measuring out 30° all the way round. Count in 30s with the class and put the numbers on the board. (Year 3 children will need marked cardboard templates to draw round, but most Year 4 children should be able to cope with using a circular protractor.) Then join the points up with a ruler to form 12 sections. Ask the children to colour in their wheel with the correct colours.

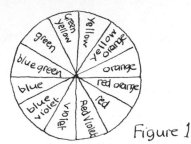

Figure 1

red
orange
yellow
green
blue
violet

Figure 2.

Computer colour

Challenge the children to make either a colour wheel or a colour layer (see Figure 2).

Science
Making rainbows

Ask the children if they know how rainbows are formed. (The sunlight splits into seven colours when shining through water.) Then make a classroom 'rainbow' (see Figure 3). If it is a sunny day, place a clear glass containing water on a window sill; a spectrum of colours should form on a sheet of plain paper placed on the floor below. If you have a prism, ask a child to cut a slit

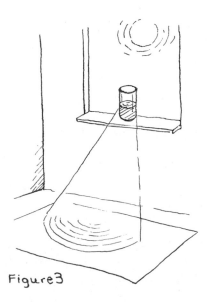

Figure 3

(letter-box fashion) in a piece of card, hold this between the light and prism and a rainbow should form. If it is a dull day, darken part of the room and place a mirror at about 30° (using Blu-Tack) in a tray of water and shine a torch on it at about 45°. A spectrum should appear on the wall. The children could then all colour an accurate rainbow.

Disappearing colours

Have a ready-made whirler to demonstrate that white light is made up of seven colours. Cut a circle of card about 6 to 8cm in diameter and divide this on both sides roughly into seven sections. Colour each section a spectrum colour in the correct order. Do the same on both sides. Make two holes in the centre of the circle about 1cm apart and push a metre length piece of string through the holes and tie the ends (see Figure 4). Flip the circle over continuously to twist up the string and then pull outwards to make the whirler spin. The whirler should appear to be white when spinning fast.

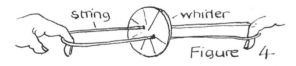

string   whirler   Figure 4

History

The English scientist, Sir Isaac Newton, discovered that he could make a spectrum by passing a narrow beam of sunlight through a triangular prism in 1665. He also discovered that by holding two prisms close together, he could pass the colour spectrum through the second prism and produce white light. You could ask some children to carry out these experiments. Explain that many colours that we see in clothes are dyes invented recently. In the past people made dyes from various fruit and vegetables.

Art and craft
Matching a colour

Invite the children to make an exact matching colour to one from a paint-strip card by mixing powder paints. Tell them to record the colours they used on their painting.

Camouflage pictures

Ask the children to each colour a picture of a creature and then add the background so that it is difficult to see it. Alternatively, ask the children each to cut out a picture of a creature from a magazine and stick this on to plain paper. Then challenge them to make appropriate camouflage backgrounds for their animals.

Music
Songs

'Yellow submarine', 'Sing a rainbow', 'Lily the pink' and 'Tiger, tiger' in *Apusskidu*
'Colours' in *Scholastic Collections: Songs*

Useful references
Information books

Colour Perception: A practical approach to colour theory T. Armstrong (1991, Tarquin Publications)
Fun with Simple Science: Colour and light B. Taylor (1991, Kingfisher)

Stories

'Particle goes green' in *Stories for Nine-Year-Olds* S. and S. Corrin (eds.) (1981, Puffin)
'King Midas' and 'Jason and the golden fleece' in *Heroes and Monsters* J. Reeves (1987, Piccolo)
'The Golden Touch' in *Stories for Seven-Year-Olds* S. and S. Corrin (eds.) (1964, Faber)
'Once there were no pandas' in *Stories Round the World* D. Grant (ed.) (1990, Hodder and Stoughton)

Poetry

Hailstones and Halibut Bones: Adventures in colour M. O'Neill (1962, World's Work)

Instant themes

Nonsense

What you need
Board and chalk; a book of Edward Lear's limericks; plain paper, pencils; photocopiable page 121; nature books; collage materials (optional); 'junk' materials, construction kits (optional).

English
Recite some nonsense poems
Write the following on the board: 'Coffee (× 2), cheese and biscuits (× 4), fruit and custard (× 6), fish and chips (× 8), sooooooooup.' The children should read the words aloud slowly and then gradually speed up. This should sound like a train. (It's a BR menu backwards!)

Limericks
If possible, read a few of Edward Lear's limericks. Discuss the rhythm pattern of limericks and then ask the children to try and make up one of their own.

Consequences
Write the following on the blackboard:
'Once upon a time there was . . .
Who lived in . . .
And liked . . .
One day . . .
And finished up . . .'.
Ask the children to work in small groups. They should copy the first phrase from the board and add what they wish. Then they should fold the paper with the writing on over so it cannot be seen and pass it on to the child beside them. Then everyone copies the next phrase and completes this, folds it over and passes it on. They should carry on like this until the last sentence is finished when the results can be read out to the class.

Maths
Nonsense sums
Put some random numbers on the board (including amounts of money and some digital times if you wish). Tell the children that these are answers and they have to write down one or more sums for each answer. Ask them to include addition, subtraction and multiplication. Challenge the Year 4 children to include some division and a simple fraction.

Nonsense day (with digital times)
Give each child a copy of photocopiable page 121. Check that the children are familiar with writing the time digitally and understand 'am' and 'pm'. (Year 4 could attempt to record their times in the 24-hour clock, if they are confident in this.) Then ask them to imagine they can have a nonsense or a backwards day. They should write the time digitally and draw the hands correctly and write underneath what they would be doing (for example 7.30 am – bedtime, 8.08 am – read in bed and so on).

Science

Weird animals and plants

Write the following on the board: 'duck-billed platypus, anteater, chameleon, Venus' fly-trap, gnu, salamander, squid.' Ask some children to find pictures of these animals and plants in books in the school library. Ask other children to see if they can find more pictures of unusual animals or plants and record anything interesting. Finish by letting the children report their discoveries.

Optical illusions

Copy a few simpler optical illusions on the board or a large sheet of paper (shown in Figure 1). Demonstrate how they are drawn and discuss them with the children who could copy them.

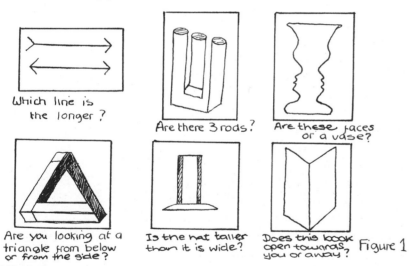

Which line is the longer?

Are there 3 rods?

Are these faces or a vase?

Are you looking at a triangle from below or from the side?

Is the hat taller than it is wide?

Does this book open towards you or away?

Figure 1

History

If the children are studying a particular period in history, ask them to find out what strange beliefs they might have had if they had lived at that time or about any odd customs.

Art and craft

Nonsense creature

Ask the children to draw or paint a fantastic creature. If you can locate any wool, material, foil or other collage materials, invite the children to add these to their picture. The children could work individually, in pairs or in a small group on a large picture.

Cartoon characters

Ask the children to sketch a crazy cartoon character or animal. They could fold a piece of A3 paper into four or six and make up a simple cartoon 'nonsense' story.

Technology

The children could work in groups, either using 'junk', modelling material or a commercial construction kit (if available) to make a nonsense machine or model.

Music

Songs

'Clementine', 'There's a hole in my bucket', 'Lily the pink', 'Michael Finnigan' and 'Down in Demerara' in *Apusskidu*
'After the ball was over' and 'Nicky, knacky, knocky, noo' in *Okki-tokki-unga*

Useful references

Stories

'Handsel and Gristle' (M. Rosen) and 'Snow-White and the seven dwarfs' (R. Dahl) in *Funny Stories* M. Rosen (ed.) (1991, Kingfisher Books)
'The road to school' in *The Boy who Bounced and Other Magic Tales* M. Mahy (1988, Puffin Books)

Poetry

The Complete Nonsense of Edward Lear J. Holbrook (ed.) (1947, Faber)
Oh, What Nonsense! W. Cole (ed.) (1990, Mammoth)
Limericks M. Palin (1986, Beaver Books)

Patterns

What you need
Board and coloured chalk, plain paper, coloured pencils or felt-tipped pens, writing pencils; dictionaries; calculators; 1cm squared paper, rulers; board ruler, scissors, cardboard, wool, needles (optional); nature books and/or natural objects; books on world religions; photocopiable page 125; examples of the work of M. C. Escher, flat, geometric shapes (e.g. hexagons); coloured sugar paper, adhesive; Multilink cubes or constructional toys (optional); tuned and untuned percussion instruments.

English
Calligrams
Calligrams are words written in the shape of the meaning of the word, so as to represent the word in some way. Write some examples on the board, in coloured chalks if possible (see Figure 1). Then encourage the children to make up their own calligrams, using coloured pencils or felt-tipped pens.

Figure 1

Word chains
Explain what a compound word is and write some examples on the board (for example 'buttercup', 'railway', 'blackbird', 'postman' and 'spaceship'). Ask the children to choose one of these words and then demonstrate on the board how to make a wordchain out of it (for example 'buttercup, cupboard, boardroom'). They should use dictionaries to help them.

Maths
Number patterns using a calculator
Write the following number patterns on the board: '50 45 40 35', '4 8 12 16 20' and '1 2 3 5 8 13'. Ask the children to work out and continue the patterns for three more figures. Then, using their calculators, ask them to make up number patterns for their friends to work out.

Curved line patterns
Draw two 50cm lines at right angles on the board. Measure out both lines into 5cm intervals. Number the vertical line from the top and the horizontal line from the joining point (see Figure 2). Then, with a board ruler, join the points with the same numbers together. The children could use 1cm squared paper (or plain paper with the lines divided into 1cm intervals). Once they have got the idea, encourage them to experiment with further designs such as squares, crosses and triangles. Alternatively, they could try out some of their designs using card, wool and a needle.

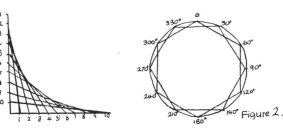

Figure 2.

Science
Ask the children to choose either a butterfly or flower to study and find a suitable book from the library or, if the weather and school environment are suitable, suggest that the children each bring in a natural object. Tell them to make an accurate, detailed drawing and a written comment about any patterns they can see.

RE

Invite the children to search for books in the library on Hinduism, Christianity, Buddhism and Islam and ask them specifically to find pictures of Diwali patterns, patterned stained-glass windows, decorated statues of Buddha and mosaics in mosques. Encourage them to copy one pattern in detail and write a little about it underneath.

Geography

Give each child a copy of photocopiable page 125. Then, using their own knowledge or books from the library, ask them to draw pictures on the map of buildings or structures with a specific pattern that they associate with that country (such as pagodas in Japan, tee-pees in the west of America and totem poles in western Canada).

Art and craft
Cut-paper patterns

Demonstrate how to take two pieces of contrastingly coloured A6 sugar paper of the same size, fold them together in half and cut sections from the folded edge. Open out and separate the pieces. Fold a piece of plain A4 paper in half. Then glue one centre piece in the middle of one half of the A4 paper. Then glue on the next size shape, but in the other colour, around it and carry on outwards. Do the same with the pieces that are left on the other half of the A4 paper (see Figure 3).

Figure 3

M. C. Escher's work

Show the children some examples of M. C. Escher's patterns, if possible. The children could attempt to design an Escher-style (tessellating) pattern. Discuss how tessellating patterns are made and let the children try drawing round hexagon shapes and colouring in their designs.

Technology

Ask the children to make a regular solid shape from cubes (or some constructional toy). Each surface must have a regular pattern. Ask the children to discuss the patterns which they make on their 3D shape.

Music
Composing using repeating patterns

Arrange the children into small groups each with a tuned percussion instrument, such as a xylophone or chime bars or an untuned percussion instrument. Ask them to use the tuned instruments to make a simple tune with no more than eight notes. Then ask them to repeat this tune, or part of it, with the percussion instruments either backing or echoing the rhythm.

Writing patterns for sounds

One way to encourage children to record their musical compositions or to write down what they have heard is to make a key for each sound (for example: ! means bang, «««« means shake, ● means rest, * means tap). Can they record the repeating pattern they have composed previously?

Useful references
Stories
The Willow Pattern Story A. Drummond (1992, North-South/Ragged Bears)

Alphabets

What you need
Board and chalk, plain paper, pencils, pens; computer; 1cm squared paper, 2cm squared paper; mirrors; books showing illuminated letters, painting materials, coloured pencils, sugar paper; books showing other alphabets; books on calligraphy; preschool alphabet books; black paint, thin brushes, book on Chinese characters; cardboard, scissors, adhesives.

English
Tongue twisters
Ask the children to make up their own tongue twisters where most of the words in the sentence must begin with the same letter, for example, 'Six sickly stick insects sticking to some string'.

Names in alphabetical order
Ask the children to write down some of their friends' names. Then tell them to rewrite the names with the surnames first. Finally, suggest that they arrange them into alphabetical order with surnames first.

Computer
Ask those children working on the computer to experiment with different fonts, sizes, styles and letter displays.

Alphabet poem
Write the following example of an alphabet poem on the board:

'A is for ants that crawl everywhere
B is for bears that wander and stare'.

Explain to the children that the theme of this poem is animals. Ask them to choose a subject of their own (such as food, places, household objects or people's names) and write a similar poem (it does not have to rhyme). Younger children could work in pairs or small groups.

Maths
Ask the children to write their first names in outline capital letters on to 1cm squared paper, making each letter 5cm high, and where possible, the strokes 1cm wide (see Figure 1). Demonstrate this on 2cm squared paper. Then ask the children to calculate the area of each letter (only concerning themselves with whole squares). Finally, ask them to add all the areas together to find the total area of their names.

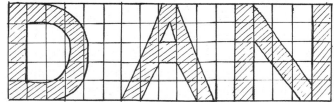

Figure 1

Science
Discuss lines of symmetry with particular reference to the symmetry of capital letters. The children could use mirrors to see which capital letters are symmetrical. They could then record and categorise the letters by their symmetry. For example: 'Totally symmetrical', 'Horizontally symmetrical' and 'Vertically symmetrical'.

RE

Explain, with particular reference to illuminated letters, how monks copied out the Bible before printing was invented. If the children can find books in the library showing illuminated letters, they could try and copy some of these or invent some of their own.

History

Ask the children to find and record some alphabets from the past (for example, Ancient Egyptian).

Geography

The children may know or could find out and then record some alphabets from other countries and compare them.
For example: Greek

α=a	η=e	ν=n	τ=t
β=b	θ=th	ξ=x	υ=u
γ=g	ι=i	o=o	φ=ph
δ=d	κ=k	π=p	χ=ch
ε=e	λ=l	ρ=r	α=ps
ζ=z	μ=m	σ/ς=s	ω=o

Art
Calligraphy

Using calligraphy books as a guide, the children could copy out the alphabet in a particular style.

Patterns using letters

Demonstrate how to make a cardboard letter template. Then ask the children to make their own, draw round this a number of times and turn this into a pattern. Alternatively, they could use commercially produced letter templates to draw round, if available.

Decorating a letter

Ask the children to do a painting, or drawing, of an enlarged letter with decoration either around or in it. Alternatively, ask them to draw an enlarged outline letter and illustrate it with items beginning with that letter (see Figure 2). They could get inspiration from reception class 'Alphabet' books.

Figure 2.

Chinese letters

Invite the children to try painting letters in a Chinese style using black paint and thin brushes. It would be helpful if you could find a book with an example.

Technology

Challenge the children to make a 3D letter from cardboard and an adhesive (see Figure 3).

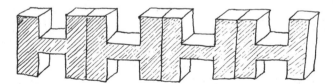

Figure 3

Useful references
Stories

'The twenty two letters' and 'The wonderful O' in *I Like This Story: A taste of fifty favourites* K. Webb (ed.) (1986, Puffin)

Poems

'A was an archer' and 'A was once in apple pie' *Faber Book of Nursery Verse* B. Ireson (ed.) (1983, Faber)
'The ABC' in *I Like This Poem: Favourite poems chosen by children* K. Webb (ed.) (1979, Puffin)

Years 5 and 6

Weather

What you need
Pencils or pens, plain paper; board and chalk; calculators; rulers, teacher-made compass-rose, protractors; water, containers, metre rulers, thermometer, compass; religious stories about the weather; photocopiable page 123; classical music tapes evoking the weather (optional).

English
Extreme weather
Ask the children to imagine that some extreme weather has hit their community, such as a hurricane, an exceptionally hot heat wave, a snow storm or a flood. Ask them to make up a story about themselves, their friends and their community in this setting.

Describing the weather
Ask the children to describe today's weather in at least three different ways:
- to make someone laugh;
- to a blind person;
- to an alien from another planet;
- as if you were a weather forecast broadcaster;
- the shortest possible way and the longest way.

Maths
Temperature conversions
Explain that 32°F is the same as 0°C (freezing point of water). Put the following conversion sums on the board:
Centigrade (C) to fahrenheit (F) is $F = \dfrac{9C}{5} + 32$

Fahrenheit (F) to centigrade (C) is $C = \dfrac{5}{9}(F - 32)$

Do an example on the board. Then write on some temperature figures (including minus numbers) and ask the children to convert these. Encourage them to do the sums conventionally and then check their answers with a calculator.

Wind direction
Draw a compass with certain degrees marked (see Figure 1) on the board. Then draw the following directional arrows: north to east ↓ ←, south to north ↑ ↓, west to north → ↓, east to south-east ← ↑, south-east to south-west ↑ ↑, and south-west to north ↑ ↓. Explain that these are meant to represent where the wind is coming from.
Then explain how to measure angles. Ask the children to draw a compass on their page and work out the angles for the change of wind direction. They could then make up some directional changes of their own.

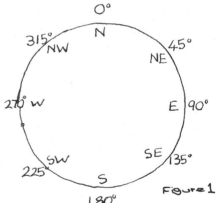

Figure 1

Science
Start this activity at the beginning of the day. Divide the children into groups and give each group responsibility for devising a set of fair tests and recording their answers.

- Evaporation group: place containers of water, each holding the same volume, in different places around the school and record the amount left at the end of the day.
- Shadow group: (if sunny) measure the length and record the direction of shadows from a set point throughout the day.
- Temperature group: record the temperature in different places in and around the school at different times during the day.
- Wind group: record the wind direction several times throughout the day.

RE
Tell the children stories from religious books involving weather, for example, Jesus calms a storm (Mark 4: 35–41).

Geography
Give each child a copy of photocopiable page 123. Ask them to devise their own weather symbols, make a key and then draw some of their symbols on the map. They could also write a written account of the weather forecast their map describes.

Art and craft
Show the children simple motifs associated with the weather and then ask them to make a colourful design for a repeating pattern. The design could be for clothes, wrapping paper, wallpaper, bed clothes or furnishings.

Music
Listen to any of the following classical pieces (or they could be played while the children are working): 'The storm' from *Pastoral Symphony* by Beethoven, *The snow is dancing* by Debussy, 'Storm' from the *William Tell Overture* by Rossini, *Four Seasons* by Vivaldi and The *Rite of Spring* by Stravinsky.

Songs
'Lots of weather' and 'Shine cold, shine hot' in *Scholastic Collections: Songs*
'The wise man and the foolish man' in *Okki-tokki-unga*
'I have seen the golden sunshine' in *Someone's singing, Lord*
'Raindrops keep falling' in *Alleluya: 77 songs for thinking people* D. Gadsby/J. Hoggarth (1990, A&C Black)
'I can see clearly now' and 'Raining in my heart' in *Juke Box: 33 pop songs* (1984, A&C Black)
'Sun arise' in *Tinder-Box: 66 songs for children* S. Barratt (ed.) (1982, A&C Black)
'Windy old weather' in *Strawberry Fair: 51 traditional songs* (1985, A&C Black)

Useful references
Stories
Necklace of Raindrops J. Aiken (1968, Cape)
Earth, Air, Fire, and Water J. Heslewood (1985, OUP)
Extract from *Sarah Plain and Tall* in *The Puffin Book of 20th Century Children's Stories* J. Elkin (ed.) (1991, Puffin)
Extract from *The Cay* in *Once Upon a Planet* J. Porritt (ed.) (1989, Puffin Books)

Poetry
Out of the Blue F. Waters (ed.) (1982, Armada)

Shopping

What you need

Board and chalk, pencils or pens, plain paper; household or gift catalogues, adhesive, scissors; calculators; large circles to draw round, rulers; photocopiable page 123, atlases; *The Trading Game* (1982, Christian Aid) (optional); newspapers, magazines; art materials; computer; sugar paper; musical instruments.

English

Events in a store

Ask the children to imagine that they witness an unusual event in a superstore or shop and ask them to write about this, in the first person. Explain that this is for an imaginary newspaper report so they will also need to think of an eye-catching headline.

Radio advert

Talk to the class about radio adverts. List on the board the important information that an advert should contain. Ask the children to consider the main focus of their advert, for example cheapness, service, choice or quality. They should then write their advert and make it as interesting as possible.

Future store

Have a class discussion first, to pool ideas, and then ask the children to write about what they think shopping will be like in the future. This could either be a written description of a store or a story.

Maths

Sale time

Explain the term 'percentage' to the class. Demonstrate on the board how to work out 10% of a price. Ask the children to cut out pictures of items and their prices from household or gift catalogues. The children should glue these on to a sheet of plain paper with the heading 'SALE 10% off'. They can then work out the new prices and write them under the originals. If any Year 5 children find the concept too hard, they could do a half price sale.

Calculating and estimating

Tell the children that they have an imaginary budget of £20 which they can spend using one catalogue (this could be either household, clothing or gifts). They should then make a record of the items they want and the prices (include postage and packing). Encourage them to make an estimate first, then add up 'long hand' and finally check their answers on a calculator. You could be more specific and indicate how many items they should buy, or state they have to buy two of one particular item.

Science

Draw a 'healthy eating wheel' on the board (see Figure 1 above) and ask the children to copy the outline on to paper. Ask them to choose menus for themselves for a day (to include breakfast, dinner and tea) and decide what items they would have to buy. Then tell them to write the various food items from their menus in the correct sections on their wheel. When they have finished, ask them to consider these meals and how they could make them more balanced on their wheel.

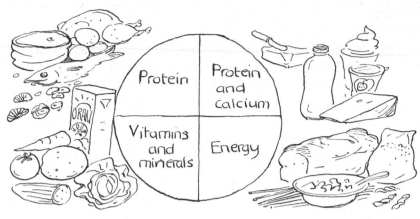

Figure 1

Geography

Give each child a copy of photocopiable page 123. Using atlases ask the children to discover names of ports and record them on their maps. They could also put a ring round their nearest port and find out how far away they are from it.

RE

Explain that many of our goods, such as tea, coffee, bananas and sugar cane and certain clothes, are produced by people in countries where the conditions are very poor and the people get very low wages. Have a class discussion or debate about how we can help; or play a game such as a simplified version of *The Trading Game* (1982, Christian Aid).

Art and craft

Design an advertisement for a store

Ask the children to look at advertisements for shops in newspapers and magazines and then design their own, producing the text on the computer.

Window dressing

Talk to the class about window dressing and what catches their eyes. Then ask the children to draw and colour or paint their own shop window for a store of their choice.

Technology

Challenge the children to make a strong bag from sugar paper, encouraging them to experiment with different shapes and adhesives.

Music

Following on from the work done in English on creating a radio advert, ask the children to turn their jingle into a song and compose some background music or sounds.

Useful references

Information books
Food and Drink (series) (1988–, Wayland)

Stories
'Film boy' in *Stories Round the World* D. Grant (ed.) (1990, Hodder & Stoughton)
'Comfort herself' in *The Puffin Book of 20th Century Children's Stories* J. Elkin (ed.) (1991, Puffin)
Extract from *The Phantom Tollbooth* in *I like this Story: A taste of fifty favourites* K. Webb (ed.) (1986, Puffin)

Poetry
A Packet of Poems: Poems about food J. Bennett (1986, OUP)
The Clever Potato: A feast of poetry for children V. Scannell (1988, Hutchinson)

Our bodies

What you need

Board and chalk, pencils or pens, plain paper; calculators, large sheets of paper; stop watches, 1cm squared paper; photocopiable page 124, dictionaries, reference books; coloured paper or card, book or picture showing internal organs; books on the origin of early humans; strong card, paper fasteners, elastic bands; percussion instruments (including xylophones and chime bars).

English
How we see each other

Write the following attributes on the board and ask the children to copy them:
- Height (tall, medium, shortish, short);
- Build (plump, average, thin, skinny);
- Hair (black, ginger, brown, blond);
- Hair style (curly, wavy, a few bends, straight);
- Eyes (blue, grey, brown, green).

Ask each child to find a partner. Ask them to, secretly, write down their partner's initial beside the attribute they think best describes him or her. Then ask them to put their own initial beside the word which best describes themselves. When everyone has done this, ask the pairs to compare their results and make a written comment on their findings. Do others perceive them as they perceive themselves?

Story about the body

This could be a story about a skeleton, a handicapped person or a science fiction style story where the body could change in some way.

Maths
Percentages

Explain how to find a percentage. Then ask the children to pick a particular criteria associated with the body (such as eye colour). Each child should then make his or her own bar chart including every child in the class. Then, using a calculator (unless the class size is an easy number to work out such as 20 or 25), tell them to work out the percentage of children in the class with each eye colour (or whatever criteria they have picked).

Pulse rate graph

Draw the pulse rates graph (see Figure 1) on the board and ask the children to copy it on to 1cm squared paper.

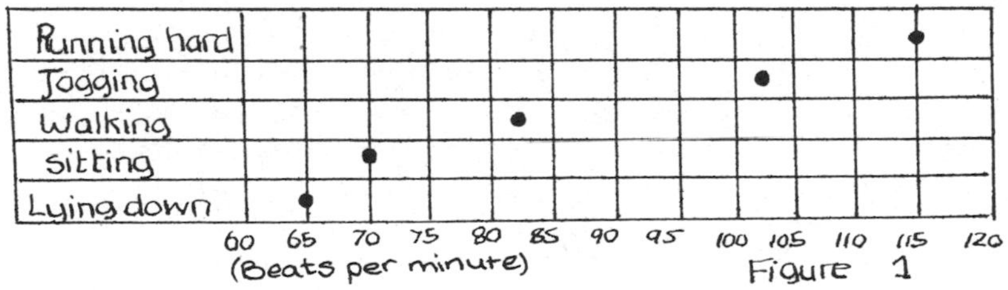

Figure 1

Show the class how to take their carotid (neck) pulse. Then ask the children to work with a friend and time each other for one minute doing the following activities: lying down, sitting up and doodling, walking on the spot, jogging steadily on the spot and running hard on the spot. After each activity, they should immediately take their pulses and plot the results on their graphs.

Science
Skeleton sheet

Give each child a copy of photocopiable page 124. Ask them to label the parts of the skeleton from their own general knowledge, dictionaries and reference books.

Our body organs

Ask the children to draw an outline of themselves on plain paper. Then tell them to draw the following organs in the positions they think they ought to be: heart, lungs, brain, liver, kidneys, stomach, bladder and intestines. Then they can compare this with a picture showing the true sizes and positions. Alternatively, they could work in groups and draw round one child on to a large piece of paper. Then draw and cut out the above organs from coloured paper or card and place them on the outline.

History

If appropriate, explain that some people think that our early ancestors were probably ape-like creatures who were much smaller than us. The children could research and draw pictures of the different stages in human development and write a short description of each underneath.

Technology

Ask the children to copy some body templates (see Figure 2) on to strong card and fix them together with paper fasteners and elastic bands. Ask them to watch what happens to the elastic bands as the arm is bent and explain that similar things happens to their muscles.

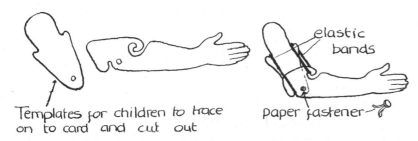

Templates for children to trace on to card and cut out

elastic bands

paper fastener

Figure 2.

Art and craft

Ask the children to make a careful, detailed, pencil sketch of one of their hands. Encourage them to keep the model hand as still as possible and to continually refer to this.

Music

Listen to 'Skeleton dance' from the film score for *Wizard of Oz* (H. Arlen) or 'Fossils' from *Carnival of the Animals* (Saint-Saëns). Arrange the class into groups and give them a variety of percussion instruments, including xylophones and chime bars. Ask them to compose their own piece around the theme of either a skeleton, giant or robot. The emphasis should be on the movement of these creatures.

Songs

'The Skeleton Stomp' and 'Dese bones a-gonna rise again' in *Swingalong Songs* S. Stevens (1981, EMI Music Publishing).
'I know they're bad for my teeth' in *Scholastic Collections: Songs*.

PE

This theme is excellent for dance work. Work on thinking about moving different parts of the body in turn and the ways they can be moved, include changing speed and slow motion movements.

Ask the children to play a favourite game but they must all only use one of their hands.

Useful references

Stories

'The fib' in *The Fib and Other Stories* G. Layton (1981, Armada)
'The Rajah's ears' in *Funny Stories* M. Rosen (ed.) (1991, Kingfisher)
Extracts from *Ramona Forever* and *The Turbulent Term of Tyke Tyler* in *The Puffin Book of 20th Century Children's Stories* J. Elkin (ed.) (1991, Puffin)

Islands

What you need
Board and chalk, plain A3 and A4 paper, coloured pencils, pencils or pens; centimetre rulers, cotton, scissors; 1cm squared paper; photocopiable page 125, atlas, art materials; empty cardboard tubes, green sugar paper; cardboard, 'junk' materials; tape-recorder, music tapes from school.

English
Journey round an island
Talk to the class about features they might find on an island: considering coastal features, vegetation, geographical areas, animals and people. Ask the children to draw a large island shape on a piece of A3 paper. Tell them to write and draw features on their islands. Then ask them to make up a story about a journey around their island, using the features they have marked.

Hidden treasure
Check that the class know the compass points. Ask the children to give a written description of where treasure is hidden on their island map. They should choose a landing spot, give directions, include paces or kilometres (see 'Maths' below) of how to get to the treasure and point out landmarks along the way.

Island facts
Ask the children working on the computer to compile a list of facts about real or their imaginary islands under the headings of: 'Name', 'Continent', 'People', 'Main town' and 'Interesting features'.

On a desert island
Ask the children to make a list of activities they would need to do to live on their island, and then sort them into priority order.

Maths
Island measurements
Using their original island (drawn on A3 paper), ask the children to make out a scale (1cm = ☐ kilometres or 1cm = ☐ metres). Then tell them to measure the length, width and the perimeter of their island, by placing cotton round the coastline and then measuring this. They could also work out the approximate area of their island by tracing it and transferring the tracing to 1cm squared paper.

Coordinates
Demonstrate to the class how to divide their island map into 5cm squares. Number the vertical lines and letter the horizontal ones (see Figure 1). Then ask them to

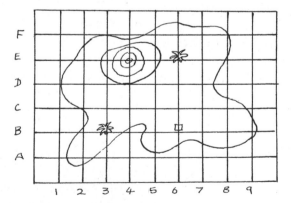

Figure 1

record the coordinates for various landmarks on their island. Some more capable children may be able to divide each square mentally into 10×10 and give very accurate coordinates.

Science

Ask the children to imagine that they are marooned on their island with only drinking water from a spring or lake. They will have to work out what food they can obtain and how to cook it (both animals and vegetables). Have a class discussion first to pool ideas, then encourage the children to research in books and record their findings.

RE

Ask the class to think about whether they would feel more religious if isolated. Encourage them to write down the kind of thoughts or prayers that might be going on in their heads in such a circumstance.

Geography

Give each child a copy of photocopiable page 125. Write the following on the board: 'West Indies', 'Canary Islands', 'Falkland Islands', 'Channel Islands', 'Hawaiian Islands', 'Galapagos Islands', 'Philippines', 'Soloman Islands', 'Bahamas', 'Balearic Islands' and 'Cayman Islands'. Then ask the children to label these groups of islands on their maps using an atlas.

Art and craft

Palm trees
Show the children how to make a simple palm tree (see Figure 2).

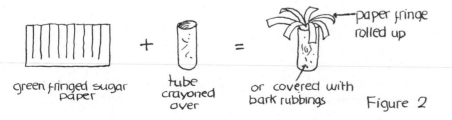

green fringed sugar paper + tube crayoned over = or covered with bark rubbings   paper fringe rolled up

Figure 2

Picture of the island

Ask the children to choose one place on their island to illustrate in detail. Alternatively, they could imagine they are looking at their island from the sea through a telescope and draw or paint what they see in a circular frame.

Technology

Ask the children to work in groups to design an island on a cardboard base. They could make palm trees and tropical flowers. Encourage them to think of ways of making different contours and geographical features on their island.

Music
Desert Island discs
Ask the children to write down their six favourite songs or pieces of music. If possible, borrow the school's tape-recorder and tapes to play the most popular pieces.

Songs
'Island in the sun' in *Ta-ra-ra boom-de-ay*
'Yellow submarine' in *Apusskidu*
'The drunken sailor' in *The Jolly Herring* R. Bush (ed.) (1980, A&C Black)
'Skye boat song' in *Strawberry Fair: 51 traditional songs* (1985, A&C Black)

Useful references
Information books
Collins Children's Atlas M. Cooper (1989, Collins)

Stories
Robinson Crusoe D. Defoe (1989, Hippo Books)
Stories Round the World D. Grant (ed.) (1990, Hodder & Stoughton)

Games

What you need

Board and chalk, board ruler, 1cm squared paper, pencils, pens; plain paper, commercial game rules; skipping ropes; calculators; teacher-made dartboard; selection of balls; books on the origins of games; card, tracing paper, scissors; adhesives, cardboard.

English
Crosswords

On the board, draw a 3×3 grid, with the centre box coloured in. Explain how a crossword is numbered and fill in the appropriate numbers. Then ask the class for a three-letter word and write this in '1 across'. Get the children to help you fill in the rest of crossword. Ask them to think of an appropriate clue for '1 across'; followed by '2 across'; then the two 'down' words. Next, give out two sheets of 1cm squared paper to each child. On one they are to write out a 3×3 crossword and on the other to draw the empty crossword with the appropriate clues. They can then try to do each others' crosswords. They may progress to making up bigger crosswords.

Rules for a game

Show the children a selection of games and rules. Ask them to design a simple game and draw up a rough outline on paper. Then encourage them to write a set of rules for their game. The children could make a neat copy of their game and illustrations. A further idea would be to ask the children to read through a set of rules for a commercial game and then tell the class the rules in their own words.

Maths
Calculator games

A game for two players and one calculator:
- child A keys in a number;
- child B keys in an operation (i.e. '+', '−', '×' or '+');
- child A keys in another number;
- child B keys in an operation ('+' or '×' if the number is below 100, '−' or '+' if above);
- child A has to finish with a number which makes 100;
- child A scores a point if she reaches 100.

The children take it in turns to be child A and child B.

Dartboard

Draw a dartboard on the board or have one previously drawn on a large sheet of paper and ask the children to copy this (see Figure 1). Explain that the centre ring scores 50, the middle ring triples the score and the outer ring doubles it. Put up on the board a random set of numbers up to 150 and ask the children to work out ways of achieving each score with three 'darts'.

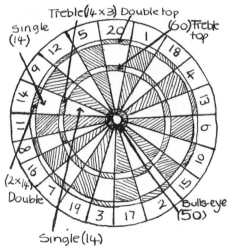

Figure 1

Science

Give the children a selection of PE balls. Tell them that they are to try and devise a fair test to see which ball bounces the highest. Suggest that they measure and record the circumference, weight, material and the bounce height of each ball. Show the tests to the class for comment.

History

Ask the children to select a favourite game and research its origins and how it has changed over the years. Alternatively, if the class are studying a particular period in history, they could find out about games played during that period.

Art and craft

Jigsaw

Ask the children to draw and colour in a picture of their choice on card (ideally something to do with games). Then ask them to trace this and make an identical outline picture. Then they can cut up the first picture into jigsaw shapes.

Action drawing

Ask one child to pose in an action shot, such as kicking a ball, a dive or holding a bat or ball. The other children can then sketch the child. Encourage them to look continually at their subject.

Technology

Ask the children to design a box for their game to go in.

PE

Ask the children to describe favourite games that they might have played with another teacher (or elsewhere). If appropriate, you could try playing these. Organise the children into small groups and first ask them to devise a simple chasing game, then a ball game and finally a game with other equipment (depending on what is available).

Skipping chants

Let the children tell you some skipping rhymes they know and ask them to think about the rhythms. Challenge them to make up their own skipping rhyme, record this and (if possible) give them a chance to try this out with a skipping rope.

Music

Play some tapes and ask the children to guess and write down what instruments are being played. Play some rhythm games, such as tapping out children's names on a percussion instrument and then well-known songs.

Songs

'Shoot! Shoot! Shoot!' in *Apusskidu*
'Football crazy' in *Jolly Herring* R. Bush (1980, A&C Black)

Useful references

Information books

Winners All: Co-operative games for all ages (1980, Pax Christi/Oxfam)

Stories

'The Fib' in *The Fib and Other Stories* G. Layton (1981, Armada)
'Mighty mountain and the three strong women' in *Stories Round the World* D. Grant (ed.) (1990, Hodder & Stoughton)

Easter customs

What you need

Pencils or pens, plain A4 paper; board and chalk; photocopiable page 119; cooking chocolate, egg, pan, cooker; books on Easter dates; books on life at the time of Jesus; world map; example of paper nun Lenten calendar; pictures or paintings of the Crucifixion by famous artists; example of quilling, strips of coloured paper (30×0.5cm), scissors, strong adhesive; skipping ropes, long rope, skittles, small bats and balls, large balls.

English

Find out how much the class knows about parts of speech by writing 'nouns', 'proper nouns', 'verbs' and 'adjectives' on the board and obtaining examples of each from the children. Then ask them to fold a piece of plain A4 paper in half. On one side they should draw a large egg and write as many words as possible associated with Easter in it. On the other side they should write the headings given on the board and categorise the words from the egg under them.

Maths

Give each child a copy of photocopiable page 119 with the following listed at the top of the sheet: 'Size 1: 70g, Size 2: 60g, Size 3: 50g, Size 4: 40g, Size 5: 30g, Size 6: 20g, egg box: 30g.'

Then ask the children to record different ways of making a full egg box weigh 300g. They can use different sizes of eggs within each box and record the egg weights within each egg shape on the sheet.

Science

If possible demonstrate melting chocolate in a pan and hard boiling an egg. Tell the children that melting the chocolate is a 'physical change' because when cool it will turn back to hard chocolate, but the egg undergoes a 'chemical change' because the change is permanent and non-reversible. Then ask the children to make a table listing the foods in recipes for Simnel cake and hot cross buns and indicate whether there would be a physical or chemical change if the ingredients were heated up individually. Set out the start of the table on the board.

	Physical change	Chemical change
Egg		✓
Water	✓	

RE

Ask the children to fold a sheet of A4 paper into six and write each title in one of the six sections: 'Ash Wednesday', 'Lent', 'Passion Sunday', 'Palm Sunday', 'Maundy Thursday' and 'Good Friday'. Then ask the children to find out about each event and record this in the appropriate section.

History

At the time of the Crucifixion life was different in many ways from today. Get the children to research one aspect of life when Jesus was alive, such as clothes, food, buildings, transport or education.

Geography

Ask the children to find out about Easter customs in other countries. Then ask them to record these and pin them on a world map.

Art and craft

French paper nun calendar

Show the children an example of the finished model. Ask them to draw and colour a nun with seven feet. Explain that the feet represent the weeks in Lent and as each week passes a foot should be folded up. (See Figure 1.)

Seven feet

(one is folded up each week in Lent)

Figure 1

Art about the Crucifixion

Show the children copies of prints of the Crucifixion by famous artists (or books with pictures of stained-glass windows depicting Easter scenes). Discuss the artists' styles, the symbolism and scenes portrayed.

Quilling

Easter cards or pictures can be made using this technique. Prepare a number of strips of coloured paper, about 30 × 0.5cm. Show the class how to twist a strip tightly round a pencil and secure the end with strong adhesive. Different shapes can be made depending on how the circle is pinched (see Figure 2).

Another technique is to fold the strip in half first and then twist from each end, either making a heart shape, 'V' or scroll shape. Encourage the children to experiment first with techniques and lay out, before sticking their strips in place.

tight coil   peardrop   Eye   leaf   heart   Scroll

Figure 2.

PE

Many games are played as part of Easter customs. Set up the playground (or hall) with different games and divide the children into groups so that they can work their way around. Skipping is traditionally associated with Easter. Try this individually and with a long rope. Set up a game of skittles, have small bats and balls in another area and finally have some large balls for the children to play handball.

Music

Songs

'Hurray for Jesus' in *Someone's singing, Lord*
'My Easter bonnet' in *Harlequin: 44 songs round the year* D. Gadsby/B. Harrop (1981, A&C Black)
'Entering Jersualem' in *Scholastic Collections: Songs*

Useful references

Information books

Bright Ideas: Easter Activities J. Fitzsimmons (1988, Scholastic)
The Easter Book J. Vaughan (1986, Macdonald)
The Easter Book F. Trotman (ed.) (1987, Hippo)
The Easter Book A. Farncombe (1984, NCEC)

Poetry

Egg Poems J. Foster (1991, OUP)

Christmas customs

What you need

Old Christmas cards, adhesive, pencils or pens, plain paper; book with traditional carols, coloured pencils or felt-tipped pens, kitchen paper, scissors; board and chalk, scales; books on Christmas customs; example of St Martin lantern, black sugar paper, coloured transparent film or tissue paper; example of Swedish heart, red and white or cream sugar paper, rulers; classical Christmas music tapes or records.

English
Inspiration from a Christmas card

Bring in some old Christmas cards and let each child choose one. They could then write a story, poem, Christmas card verse or a descriptive piece of writing using the card for ideas. If you do not wish to keep the cards, these could be stuck alongside their work.

Christmas carols

Ask the children to choose a traditional carol and copy this out one verse at a time. Under each verse they should write their own interpretation of the words. The carol could be written in coloured pencil or felt-tipped pen. Some children might wish to write their own Christmas carol.

Maths
Finding the area of wrapping paper

Remind the class how to find the area of a rectangle. Ask the children to choose something portable in the classroom that is an awkward shape and to imagine that they are giving this as a present. Then get them to cut out a rectangle of kitchen paper big enough to wrap the present and then find the area of their paper. This activity could be extended for some children by asking them to wrap up presents using a triangular-shaped piece of kitchen paper.

Costing parcels

Write the following table on the board.

Weight	UK	Europe	America	Australia
1kg	£2.50	£9.70	£10.50	£14.20
2kg	£3.15	£11.30	£14.50	£18.60
3kg	£4.10	£12.90	£18.50	£23.00
4kg	£6.25	£14.50	£22.50	£27.40
5kg	£7.80	£16.10	£26.50	£31.80

Ask the children to choose an object from the classroom and imagine that they are sending it as a present. They will then need to weigh it, choose where they will send it and cost this out. (Alternatively, bring in some Post Office parcel post leaflets and ask the children to find out the relevant information for themselves.)

Science

Many homes are decorated with evergreens at Christmas. Ask the children to make a list of evergreen trees and shrubs. Then ask them to note any similarities and see if they can deduce why they keep their leaves in winter.

History

Ask the children to choose one or two Christmas customs and find out their origins using reference books to help.

RE

Ask the children to imagine that they are a shepherd, wise man or an animal in the stable and retell the Christmas story in writing from that point of view. Alternatively, ask the children to write and illustrate the Christmas story for a very young child.

Art and craft
St Martin lantern (Germany)

Ask the children to fold a strip of black sugar paper or card (42×15cm, half A3) into four. Then help them to cut out Christmas shapes (such as trees, bells and stars) from the four sections and stick some coloured transparent film or tissue paper behind the gaps. Finally they should glue the lantern into shape (see Figure 1). A simpler, circular version can be made by cutting squares from the strip, gluing cellophane behind and gluing the strip as shown. Some children may wish to make a light to go inside their lantern (see Years 1 and 2 'Homes' theme).

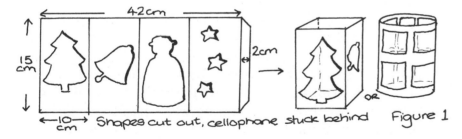

Shapes cut out, cellophane stuck behind. Figure 1

Swedish hearts

Give each child two rectangles (half A4 size, 30×10cm) of different colours. They should fold the two rectangles together and cut a curve at the open end (see Figure 2). Then, tell them to draw 4 parallel lines as shown and cut along these and then separate the shapes and hold them (still folded) at right angles to each other. Weave the strips of the shapes through and around each other until a heart-shaped basket is formed.

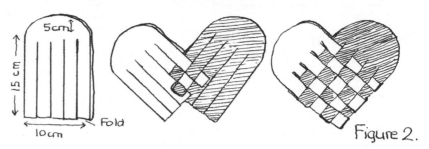

Figure 2.

Music

Let the children listen to some classical Christmas music such as *A Classic Christmas* (EMI). This could be played while the children are doing their Christmas activities.

Useful references

Songbooks
Carol Gaily Carol: Christmas songs for children B. Harrop (ed.) (1979, A&C Black)
Merrily to Bethlehem: A very unusual carol book D. Gadsby/ I. Golby (eds.) (1979, A&C Black)

Information books
Christmas Customs D. Miller (1988, Ladybird)
Inspirations for Christmas J. Jones (1991, Scholastic)
Merry Christmas S. Ichikawa (1983, Heinemann)
Scholastic Collections: Christmas P. Gooch (comp.) (1992, Scholastic)

Stories
The Puffin Book of Christmas Stories S. and S. Corrin (1986, Puffin)
'The Christmas party' in *The Fib and Other Stories* G. Layton (1991, Armada)
'The great white cat' in *Stories Round the World* D. Grant (ed.) (1990, Hodder & Stoughton)

Poetry
The Oxford Book of Christmas Poems M. Harrison/C. Stuart-Clarke (1988, OUP)

Ancient Egypt

What you need

Board and chalk, plain paper, pencils or pens, books on Ancient Egypt; solid square-based pyramid shape; photocopiable page 124, coloured pencils, scissors, adhesive tape; pictures and information about Egyptian gods; atlases, tracing paper; powder paints, sugar paper; cardboard, black sugar paper, stapler; felt-tipped pens, shiny paper; constructional bricks such as LEGO; cardboard, crayons, adhesives, empty toilet rolls, green sugar paper.

English
Hieroglyphs

Show the children some Egyptian hieroglyphs (see Figure 1). Ask them to design some of their own and then put them together to make a sentence.

Nose / Joy	Precious metal	Wood	Motion	Woman / Female

Figure 1

Pyramid poem

Ask the children to write a poem about Ancient Egyptians or pyramids but in the shape of a pyramid. Tell them to start with just one or two words and then make each line progressively longer, for example:

Long
Long Ago
The Ancient Egyptians
Built extraordinary structures
In the hope of keeping their kings immortal.

Maths

Show the children some solid 'square-based' pyramids. Check that they understand what an 'equilateral' triangle is. Then ask them to make their own 3D pyramid from plain paper, with a square base and four equilateral triangles. You may wish to put an example on the board or let the children work this out for themselves (see Figure 2).

Paper Pyramid

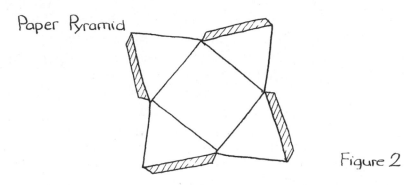

Figure 2

Science

Explain that mummies were preserved by being dried out. Certain organs were removed, then the body was washed and dried, rubbed with oil, bandaged and buried. Give each child a copy of photocopiable page 124. Ask the children to cut out the skeleton and then cut out four pieces of white 'tomb-shaped' paper the same size as this. On one they should draw a body with a heart in and on the next draw a swaddled mummy, the next should show a decorated anthropoid (mummy-shaped coffin) that is slightly bigger than the bodies, and finally they should draw a sarcophagus decorated with gods and hieroglyphs. Each figure should be slightly larger than the previous one. Ask the children to fasten the pieces together (in the correct order) with a piece of adhesive tape (see Figure 3).

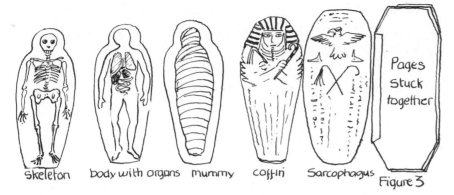

skeleton   body with organs   mummy   coffin   Sarcophagus   Figure 3

RE

Encourage the children to draw pictures of and find out about Egyptian gods. The most important family were Osiris (king of the afterworld), Isis his wife, Horus their son and Seth (the brother of Osiris and god of evil). Other well-known gods were Anubis (a jackal-headed god of the afterworld) and Sekhmet (with the head of a lioness).

History

Ask the children to research into one aspect of Ancient Egypt that particularly interests them. You could suggest clothes, jewellery and make-up, homes, animals, education or building a pyramid.

Geography

Ask the children to either copy or trace a map of Egypt, marking in the Red Sea, the Nile, Alexandria, Cairo, El Giza, Luxor and Aswan. Let the children also mark places that were important in Ancient Egypt in a distinctive way on their maps, such as Tanis, Heliopolis, Memphis, Hermapolis, Abydos, Edfu, Elephantine, Abu Simnel and Napata (if you have access to this information).

Art and craft
Paintings in Egyptian style

Show the class some stylised Ancient Egyptian paintings. Then ask the children to work in groups to paint or draw and colour in a frieze with Egyptian people, gods and animals shown in profile.

Wigs and head-dresses

Show the children how to make a cardboard band to fit around their heads and staple on some fringed black sugar paper to make a wig. An animal god head-dress could be added if two head profiles are stapled on to either side of the wig and then stapled at the nose.

Jewellery

Some children might enjoy making Egyptian amulets or decorated collars from card, using felt-tipped pens and shiny paper for decoration.

Technology
Pyramids

Challenge the children to make a pyramid with a constructional toy such as LEGO.

Pyramid scene

Ask the children to make 3D pyramids from card and make a scene by painting a base representing sand and the river. Palm trees could be added (see Years 5 and 6 'Islands' theme).

Useful references
Information books

People of the Past: The Egyptians A. Millard (1978, Macdonald)
Ancient Egyptians Activity Book L. Manniche (1985, British Museum Publications)
Gods and Pharaohs from Egyptian Mythology G. Harris (1982, Peter Lowe)

Communication

What you need

Books containing sign language, Braille and Morse codes, pencils or pens, plain paper; board and chalk; batteries, bulbs, crocodile leads, simple switch; books on different religions; books on inventions; Ordnance Survey maps; pictures of abstract art; examples of logos, magazines; a highway code book, cardboard, 'junk' material.

English

Sign language, Braille and Morse code

Ask the children to research the codes people use such as Braille, Morse and sign language. Discuss each code and when it is used. Tell the children to select one of the codes and construct their name and a simple message in that code. Ask them to decipher each other's messages. Challenge them to produce a Braille message in raised or indented dots.

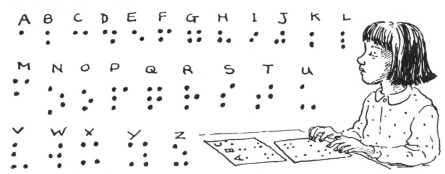

Telephone conversation

Show the children how to use speech marks. Then ask them to write an imaginary telephone conversation using this convention.

Maths

Explain to the children that not everyone uses base 10 or our numerical symbols.

Write some Roman numerals on the board and show how larger numbers were constructed. A smaller value symbol only ever appears before a larger value symbol when it is to be subtracted. For example:

MDCLXVI = 1000 + 500 + 100 + 50 + 10 + 5 + 1 = 1666
MCMLXXVI = 1000 + (1000 − 100) + 50 + 10 + 10 + 5 + 1 = 1976

Tell the children how calculators and computers use base 2, the binary system, and convert all their information into strings of zeros and ones.

Historically, the Mayan people used base 20, with a line for each group of 5 and a dot for each unit. Place value was indicated vertically. The arrangement for numbers up to 20 is given below.

Invent some simple sums for the children, or challenge them to set problems for each other, using one of these systems. Alternatively, ask them to research other number and counting systems; for example, 12d was 1 shilling.

Science

Using the example shown of how to make a light switch, in 'Science', Years 3 and 4 'Lights' theme, the children could make their own signalling devices and then signal to each other perhaps using Morse code (see below).

A • –	B –•••	C –•–•	D –••	E •	F ••–•
G ––•	H ••••	I ••	J •–––	K –•–	L •–••
M ––	N –•	O –––	P •––•	Q ––•–	R •–•
S •••	T –	U ••–	V •••–	W •––	X –••–
Y –•––	Z ––••				

RE

Encourage the children to research the symbols used in different religions and why they are used (see Figure 1).

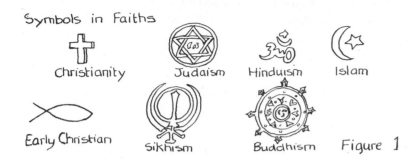

Figure 1

History

Ask the children to find out who invented the different types of communication, for example the television, radio, telephone and printing. Discuss the history of writing from cave paintings, to papyrus and clay tablets, to quill pens, biros and word processors.

Geography

Show the children some symbols used on Ordnance Survey maps. Ask them to copy the symbols and then guess what they represent. Give them an Ordnance Survey map to check their guesses.

Art and craft

Logos

Show the class some examples of logos. Ask them to find more examples of logos from magazines and books and copy them. They could record the manufacturer's or publisher's name alongside each picture and state whether they think the logo is effective. Some children may enjoy designing a logo for their school or an imaginary business they would like to run.

Abstracts

Show the children some examples of abstract art. Ask them to write about what they think was in the artist's mind when producing the work and what they think the artist wished to communicate through it.

Technology

Show the children some road signs in a highway code book and explain the difference between warnings and compulsory order signs. Challenge the children to make an automatic stop/go sign. The sign should be self-supporting and designed so that it can be operated from a few metres away.

PE and drama

Tell the children that they are going to 'mime' and communicate without saying anything. First, ask the children to concentrate on communicating with facial expressions, then using body language and finally using movement. Ask the children to work in pairs and imagine that one of them is in a foreign country but cannot speak the local language. They should act out a scene in which one of them asks for something from the other. Then have the whole class imagine that one group are aliens trying to communicate with the other group, who are humans.

Useful references

Stories

Fingers crossed: Stories for nine-year-olds (section entitled 'Words') C. Powling (ed.) (1988, Knight Books)
'The fib' in *The Fib and Other Stories* G. Layton (1981, Armada)
'The great sea serpent' in *Funny Stories* M. Rosen (ed.) (1991, Kingfisher)
'The first letter' in *Just So Stories* R. Kipling (1991, Armada Classics)

Poetry

Cohen's Cornucopia to Twist the Tongue and Jerk the Jaw M. Cohen (ed.) (1983, Patrick Hardy Books)

Instant themes

An ideal world

What you need

Plain paper, pencils or pens; books on famous inventors; photocopiable page 125, atlases (optional); A3 paper or sugar paper, painting materials; 'junk' materials, card, various textures of paper, wool and material (optional), scissors, adhesives.

English
An ideal world in the future

Ask the children to imagine a world in the future which they consider would be ideal for everyone. Ask them to outline the way of life first and then write a story.

Happiness

Ask the children to consider what happiness means to different people, or to various creatures, or anything else that takes their imagination, and then try to sum up their ideas as a poem.

An ideal day

Ask the children to imagine they can do exactly what they want for a day. They should set out their day as a timetable, writing the times down the left-hand side of the paper. Their ideas must be realistic and set in the present. You could also stipulate that they set off from their home but they have an unlimited amount of money.
For example:
8.00 Wake up, lie in bed reading my favourite comics.
8.30 Get up and have an enormous breakfast of cereal, bacon and sausage . . . .

Maths

Tell the children they are to imagine that they have £5 per week pocket money (or more perhaps!) and they can spend it as they wish. Ask them to set out a table to show roughly how they would choose to spend it. Then ask them to work out how much they would have after five years if they saved all of it and put it in a bank where the interest rate is 10%.

Science
Ideal weather

Ask the children to imagine that they can plan ideal weather for this country. Ask them to consider not only their own enjoyment, but what vegetation and animals they would like to have.

Ideal menu for a day

Ask the children to write out an ideal menu for a day and then check how healthy this would be (see Years 5 and 6 'Shopping' theme).

RE

Ask the children how they can help to make the world a better place in their own way. Suggest that they plan to help one of their friends, help in the classroom and help at home during the day. Then invite them to work in groups or pairs to think about helping in their community or raising money to help people less fortunate than themselves.

History

List the following people on the board and ask the children to choose one and find out as much as possible about them: Newton, Einstein, Gallileo, Stevenson, Bell, Ford, Marconi, Baird. Spend some time putting together all the children's information into profiles of the various inventors.

Geography

Give each child a copy of photocopiable page 125. Ask them to mark places where they would like to see changes. Then ask them to either write about these on the map or on a separate piece of paper. Encourage them to consider environmental and social problems.

Art and craft
Poster

The children could design a poster to encourage people to make the world a better place. This could be anti-litter or a request to save rainforests or animals from extinction or to help handicapped or starving people.

World of the future

Ask the children to sketch or paint a picture of a future world. They could concentrate on one particular issue such as transport, housing or clothing.

Litter collage or picture

Ask the children to draw a large picture of a scarecrow or dustbin and then stick on pieces of junk, card, various textures of paper, wool and material, if available (see Figure 1).

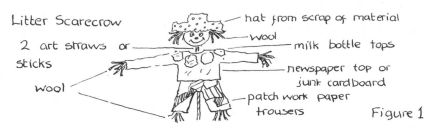

Litter Scarecrow — hat from scrap of material — wool — milk bottle tops — newspaper top or junk cardboard — patch work paper trousers — 2 art straws or sticks — wool

Figure 1

Technology

Ask the children to design and make a litter receptacle, either with different compartments for different kinds of litter or with some way of compressing the litter. They should use 'junk' materials available in the classroom and they could work in pairs or small groups.

PE

Ask the children what their ideal PE lesson would be and then have a democratic vote on selecting activities. Follow the activities up if school resources allow.

Music

Listen to New World Symphony Nos. 8 and 9 (Dvořák).

Songs

'The world we live in' in Scholastic Collections: Songs 'Milk bottle tops and paper bags' and 'Think of a world without any flowers' in Someone's singing, Lord

Useful references
Stories
'Under Plum Lake' in I Like This Story: A taste of fifty favourites K. Webb (ed.) (1986, Puffin)

Time

What you need

Plain paper, pencils, pens; board and chalk; photocopiable page 121; rulers, board ruler; board protractor, circular protractors; weights, string, stop-watches or watches with second hands; photocopiable page 125, atlases; painting materials or pastels, charcoal; paper fasteners, cardboard; 'junk' materials, adhesives.

English
The amazing clock

Ask the children to write a story in which they find a magical clock which can either take them forwards or backwards in time. Ask the children to choose a place and time to visit and write details of what they see.

Choose a time

Ask the children to choose a time of day, for example night time. Suggest that they jot down all the ideas that they can think of to do with the time they have chosen, including things they might see and hear and how they feel. Then they could compose their thoughts into a poem.

Maths
24-hour clock

Give each child a copy of photocopiable page 121. Write the following on the board: 01:15, 03:05, 10:54, 13:09, 16:22, 19:48 and 23:56. Then ask the children to write these times under the clocks on their sheet, draw in the hands and also write the time in words.

Drawing a clock face accurately

Explain that you want the children to draw an accurate clock face. Demonstrate on the board, using a board protractor, how to divide a circle into 30° divisions and write in the figures (see Figure 1). Then ask the children to do the same using circular protractors. (Year 6 children could attempt to put in the minute marks too).

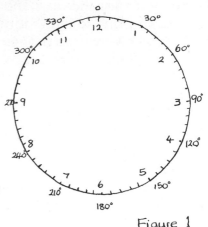

Figure 1

Timetables

Write the following on the board (change the place names for local places).

London	6:00	11:05	14:10	18:20
Chelmsford	6:20	11:25		18:40
Colchester	6:45	11:50		19:05
Ipswich	7:03	12:08	14:50	19:22
Stowmarket	7:11	12:16		19:30
Norwich	7:48	12:53	15:30	20:07

Ask the children to copy this and then answer the following questions.
- Work out the time differences between the stations on the first train, for example Chelmsford to Colchester.
- Work out the time of the journeys between each station and London.
- The next train after the 18:20 from London runs half an hour later. Work out the times it will stop at all the stations.

Science

Invite the children to make a pendulum by tying a weight to the end of a piece of string. Hang the pendulum so that it can swing freely. Then ask the children to count and record the number of swings the pendulum makes in one minute. Suggest that the children experiment with letting the pendulum drop from different heights and then with lengthening and shortening the string. They should record their findings.

Geography

Give each child a copy of photocopiable page 125. Ask the children to divide their maps vertically into 1cm sections with a ruler. (The map is 24cm across so there should be no problem). The 0° line of longitude through London (00:00) and the 180° line (12:00) are already indicated. Explain that the time in those countries to the right of the 0° line is one or more hours ahead of us and in those to the left is one or more hours behind. Explain about the International Date Line at 180°. Ask the children to write the current time over the 0° line. Write these places on the board: Rome, Los Angeles, Oslo, Moscow, Tokyo, Toronto, Sydney, Cairo, New York, Rio de Janeiro, Bombay, Hawaii and Falkland Islands. Ask the children to find these places in atlases, mark them on their maps and then work out what the time is in these places.

Art and craft
Sunset and sunrise pictures

Ask the children to use paint (or pastels) to create a background of reds, oranges and purples. Then, in the foreground, ask them to draw silhouettes in charcoal.

Life-cycle or seasonal change pictures

Ask the children to fold a sheet of A4 paper into four.

Then ask them to choose either an animal or plant and draw each stage of its development (or seasonal changes) in one of the four sections. Some children might turn this into a 'life-cycle wheel' (see Figure 2).

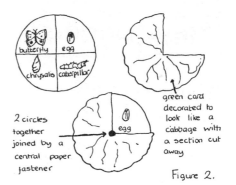

Figure 2.

Technology

Challenge the children to design a 3D clock to include moving hands. This could be the clock described in their story (see 'English') and they could use the accurate clock face drawn in 'Maths'. Suggest the use of paper fasteners to attach the hands.

Music
Time signatures

Write the following on the board: crochet=1 beat; minim (2 crochets)=2 beats; semibreve (4 crochets)=4 beats; quaver (half a crochet)=$\frac{1}{2}$ beat. Explain that all pieces of music have a 'time signature' which indicates how many beats there are in a bar. Write $\frac{4}{4}$ on the board and explain that this means four crochets in a bar. Demonstrate other combinations for $\frac{4}{4}$ and help the class to clap out the rhythms. Then ask the children to make up and write down their own rhythms using a $\frac{4}{4}$ time signature. They could try out their rhythms on percussion instruments. Some children may wish to move on to $\frac{3}{4}$ time signatures.

Useful references
Stories

Extracts from *Tom's Midnight Garden* and *Stig of the Dump* in *Puffin Book of 20th Century Children's Stories* J. Elkin (ed.) (1991, Puffin)

Newspapers

What you need

Large sheets of white paper, scissors, adhesive, lined and plain paper, pencils or pens, computer or typewriter (optional); calculator; old newspapers, atlases, tracing paper (optional); transfer lettering (optional); adhesive tape.

English

The children could choose any of the ideas below and their efforts could be mounted on large sheets of white paper in columns to form a class newspaper (see Figure 1). Put the headings on the board for the children to choose from.

Imaginary newspaper report

Ask the children to imagine that some extraordinary event has happened either in their home, school or local community. They are to write an account of this, either in the first person or as a report.

An interview

Ask the children to make up some questions to ask either a friend or someone working in the school (check at playtime if this is convenient). They could then write a report using their information.

What's on

Make a diary of school events for the week including class assemblies, clubs and activities and visitors. Roaming reporters could find out what themes other classes are covering this week.

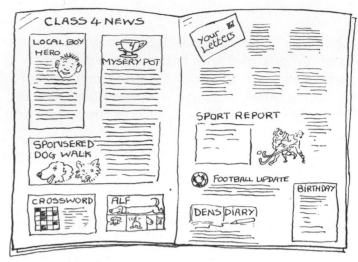

Figure 1

Letter to the editor

Remind the children about how to set out a letter and suggest that they write 'to the editor' about something that may be concerning them, for example school dinners, uniform, environmental issues and so on.

Story using a newspaper photograph

Ask the children to cut a picture from a newspaper and then ask them to write a story about it without referring to the original report.

Sports report

Some children could report on a recent school or local match.

Computer publishing

Many schools will have a specific newspaper program such as *Caxton Press* (for Nimbus computers). A sample of each of the newspaper's sections could be typed out by the authors.

Maths
Production costs of a newspaper
Ask the children to pick a newspaper, note the cost and the circulation figure. Then multiply the figures together to find the total. Write the following on the board: 'Advertising 5%', 'Writers' fees 50%', 'Producing paper 20%', 'Delivery 5%' and 'Newsprint 1%'. Ask the children to work out the production costs using a calculator (if necessary) and the profit to the owner.

Newspaper survey
Some children could note the names of newspapers bought by households in the class and then make a pictorial representation of this, such as a bar graph or pie chart.

Science
Challenge the children to test the quality of newsprint. Ask them to work in groups and devise a fair test for either how easily the ink runs, how waterproof the paper is or how strong the paper is. They should work systematically and record their results.

History
If the children are studying a particular period of history, ask them to imagine that they have discovered an artefact from the period. They should draw pictures and write a report about the artefact and its use.

Geography
If the class are studying a particular country they could find articles about it in newspapers. They could then copy or trace a map of the country and paste the articles around this.

RE
Ask the children to find and cut out of newspapers any articles about religion and paste these together on a sheet of paper.

They could also write reports of any recent religious celebrations for the class newspaper.

Art and craft
Cartoons
Some children will enjoy devising their own cartoon characters and sketches. Encourage them to look at newspaper cartoons first.

Advertisements
Encourage the children to look through the old newspapers first to see how adverts are set out. They could use the computer, the typewriter or transfer lettering, if available.

Music
Songs
'It's our job (The media song)' in *Scholastic Collections: Songs*

Useful references
Stories
'Sniff makes the news' in *The Sniff Stories* I. Whybrow (1990, Red Fox)

Poems
'Advertising' and 'Here is the news' in *Wouldn't You Like to Know* M. Rosen (1981, Puffin)

Part 3 — reproducible material and resources

Balances, see pages 18 and 32

Title:

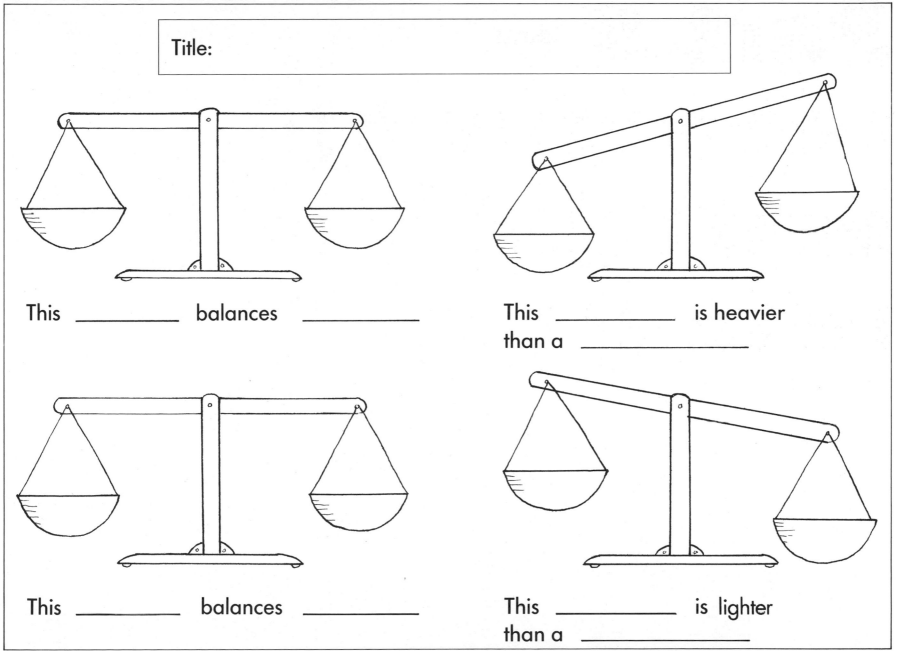

This _____ balances _____

This _____ is heavier than a _____

This _____ balances _____

This _____ is lighter than a _____

This page may be photocopied for use in the classroom and should not be declared in any return in respect of any photocopying licence.

Toys, see pages 20, 38 and 64

This page may be photocopied for use in the classroom and should not be declared in any return in respect of any photocopying licence.

Fruit and vegetables, see pages 22, 36, 38 and 42

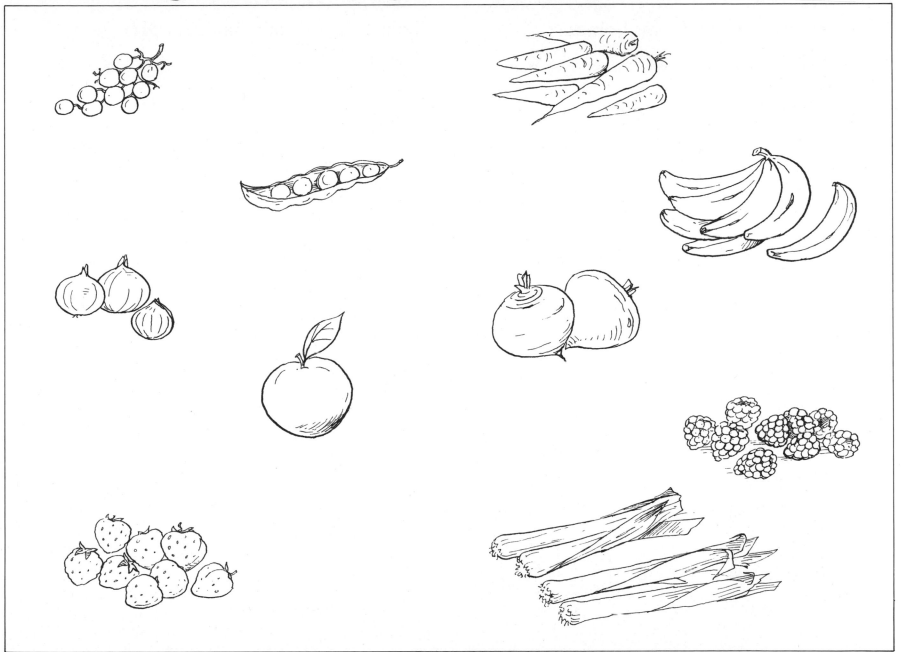

This page may be photocopied for use in the classroom and should not be declared in any return in respect of any photocopying licence.

Farm animals and their homes

- Draw a line to join each animal to its home.

horse

pond

duck

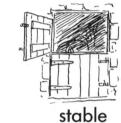

stable

dog

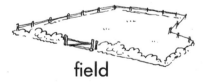

field

goat

kennel

Farm animals and their products

- Draw a line from each animal to the product we get from it.

cow

eggs

hen

wool

pig

milk

sheep

bacon

This page may be photocopied for use in the classroom and should not be declared in any return in respect of any photocopying licence.

Egg boxes, see pages 28, 78 and 100

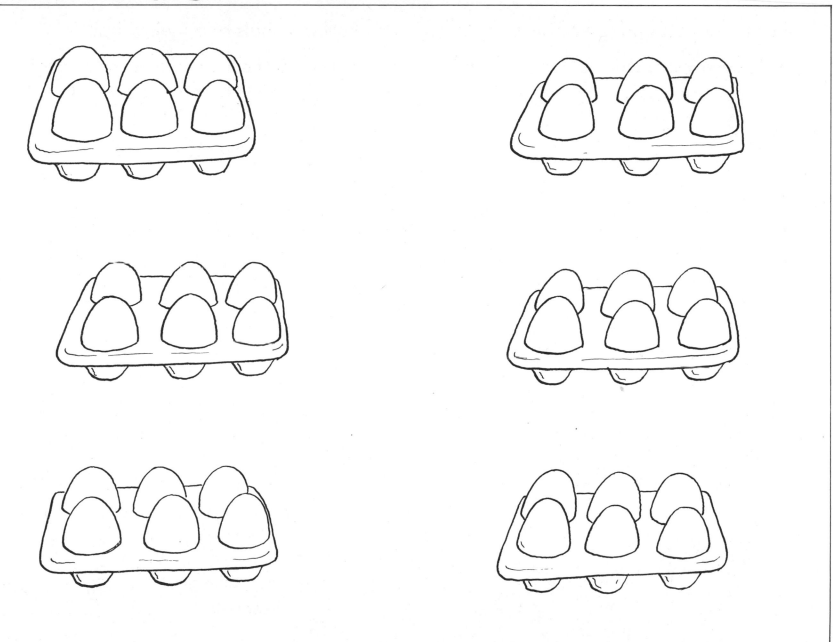

This page may be photocopied for use in the classroom and should not be declared in any return in respect of any photocopying licence.

Homes, see pages 49, 61, 65 and 73

This page may be photocopied for use in the classroom and should not be declared in any return in respect of any photocopying licence.

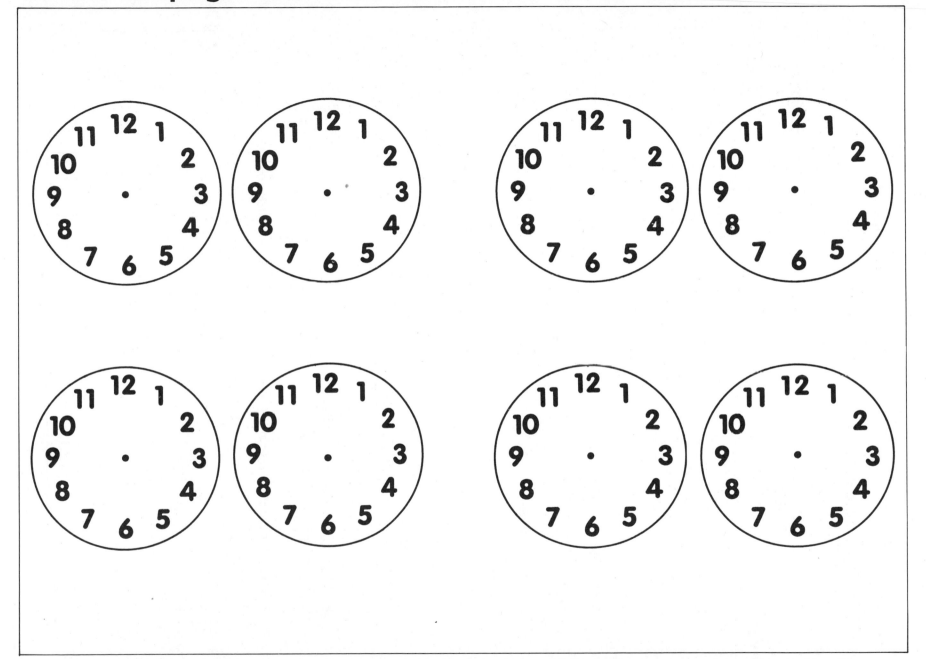

This page may be photocopied for use in the classroom and should not be declared in any return in respect of any photocopying licence.

How we travel to school, see page 56

How we travel to school

- How many children in your class come to school in each of the following ways:

by train?

by car?

by taxi?

by bus?

by bike?

by walking?

- Most children in my class travel to school by:

- Draw yourself travelling to school in the box below.

This page may be photocopied for use in the classroom and should not be declared in any return in respect of any photocopying licence.

United Kingdom map, see pages 91 and 93

This page may be photocopied for use in the classroom and should not be declared in any return in respect of any photocopying licence.

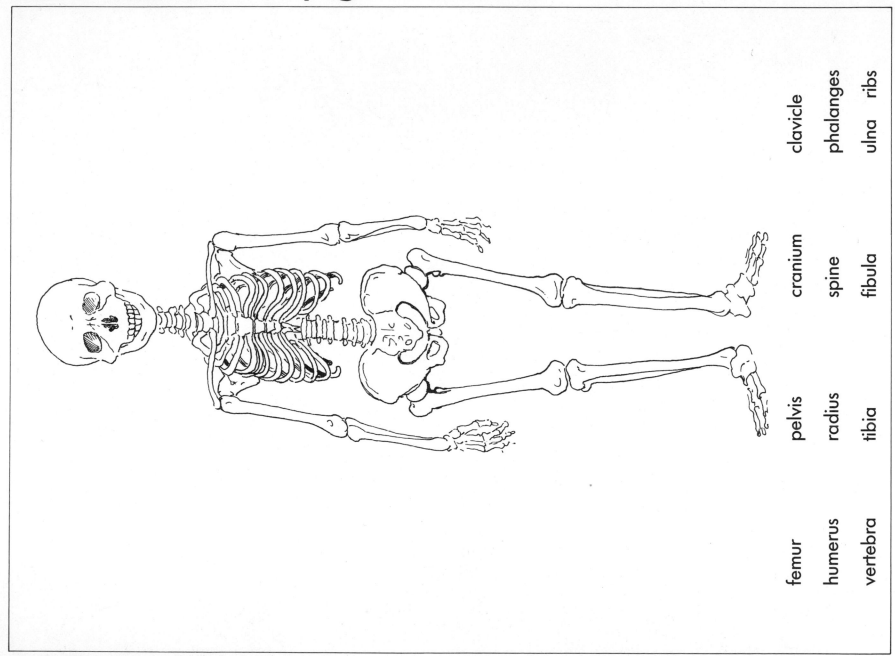

clavicle
phalanges
ulna ribs

cranium
spine
fibula

pelvis
radius
tibia

femur
humerus
vertebra

This page may be photocopied for use in the classroom and should not be declared in any return in respect of any photocopying licence.

World map, see pages 86, 97, 109 and 111

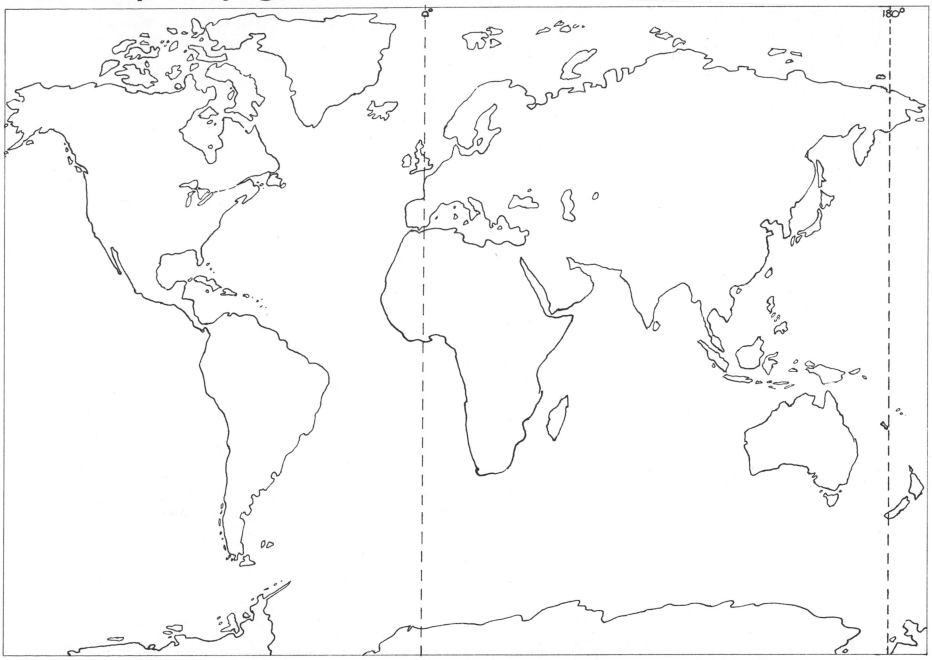

This page may be photocopied for use in the classroom and should not be declared in any return in respect of any photocopying licence.

RECOMMENDED READING
Song and poetry books
Many of the songs and rhymes listed come from the following:
Apusskidu B. Harrop (ed.) (1975, A&C Black)
The Nursery Rhyme Book (1979, Wise Publications)
Okki-tokki-unga B. Harrop (ed.) (1976, A&C Black)
Scholastic Collections: Songs P. Morrell (comp.) (1992, Scholastic)
Someone's singing, Lord B. Harrop (ed.) (1973, A&C Black)
Ta-ra-ra Boom-de-ay D. Gadsby/B. Harrop (eds.) (1977, A&C Black)
This Little Puffin: Finger plays and nursery games E. M. Matterson (1991, Puffin)

Classroom management and curriculum books
All about the National Curriculum C. Emerson/ I. Goddard (1989, Heinemann Educational)
The National Curriculum: A survival guide for parents R. Merttens/J. Vass (1989, Heinemann Educational)
A Parent's Guide to the New Curriculum M. Baker (1992, BBC)
You Know the Fair Rule B. Rogers (1991, Longman)

Supply teaching and subject books
Bright Ideas: Lifesavers D. Montgomery/ A. Rawlings/N. Hadfield (1987, Scholastic)
Goldmine D. Brown (1989, David Brown, PO Box 9, Heathfield, Sussex TN21 0DN)
Green Guide to Children's Books R. Hill (1991, Books for Keeps)
Primary Teacher's Handbook M. R. Selman/M. Baird (1986, Oliver & Boyd)
Stand-by K. Blackford/J. Humphries (1980, Arnold Wheaton)
366 Emergency Ideas for Every Day of the Year: Ideas for teachers V. Ferguson/P. Durkin (1990, Oliver & Boyd)
English
Blue Prints: English (Key stage 1 copymasters) J. Fitzsimmons/R. Whiteford (1991, Stanley Thornes)
Bright Ideas: Spelling D. Bentley (1987, Scholastic)
Bright Ideas: Writing D. Wray (1987, Scholastic)
The First Poetry Book J. Foster (ed.) (1979, OUP)
Picture Word Book 5–7 K. Howard (1984, Holmes MacDougall)
Word Play: Primary language course D. Taylor (1984, CUP)
Maths
100's of Ideas for Primary Maths P. Harding (1990, Hodder & Stoughton)

Science
Blue prints: Science 5–7 J. Fitzsimmons/R. Whiteford (1990, Stanley Thorne)
An Early Start to Science R. Richards et al (1989, Simon & Schuster)
EC007 Handbook for Life and *EC001 Electricity* (Understanding Electricity)
RE
Ladybird Bible Storybook J. Robertson/O. Hunkin (Yorkshire TV) (1983, SU/Ladybird Books)
101 School Assembly Stories F. Carr (1973, W. Foulsham & Co.)
Geography
Collin's Children's Atlas (1989, Collins)
Map of the World (Peter's Projection) Christian Aid
Art
Simply Artistic J. Chambers/M. Hood (1988, Belair)
Technology
An Early Start to Technology R. Richards (1990, Simon & Schuster)

THEMATIC RESOURCES
Any additional classroom equipment needs can be obtained from educational suppliers, e.g. NES/ Arnold, Hope, Philip and Tacey, CRAFTPACKS, Galt, LDA, Taskmaster, TTS and PCET. See the 'Useful addresses'.

Reception
Seaside
'Seashore' wrapping paper – Medici
'The rockpool' wooden animal templates – WATCH
Coloured sand (10 assorted bags of sand) – Hope or NES/Arnold
Toys
'In the park' (poster – children playing with Victorian outdoor toys) – Medici
Starting History: Children (project pack) (1992, Scholastic)
Food
'Where does our food come from?' (poster) – Christian Aid
'The milk story' (free poster) and *Ourselves* (free pack) – Milk Marketing Board
Good Things to Eat (free booklet) and 'Milk from earliest times' (poster) – National Dairy Council
The Banana Story (video and poster) – Banana Group Education Service
Flowers
'Summer garden' wrapping paper – Medici
Farm animals
Fleeces – British Wool Marketing Board
'Toy farm' wrapping paper – Medici
Up From the Country (free booklet) – National Dairy Council

Easter
'The Egg Story' (free wallchart and activity cards), *Food For All* (free project pack) and *Exploring Eggs* (video) – British Egg/Chicken Informational Service
Easter festival stamps – Philip and Tacey
Palm Sunday and Easter (freize) – NCEC
Clothes
Silk cocoon, samples of silk yarn and fabric – Silk Education Service
Yarns for fashion and furnishing (free samples of 12 different types of wool) and Fabrics for fashion (free samples of 9 different wool fabrics) – CBWT
Sample pack for experimentation (wools) – British Wool Marketing Board
'What should I wear?' (poster) – RoSPA
Starting History: Children (project pack) (1992, Scholastic)
Preparing for Christmas
'Christmas' (freize) – NCEC
Christmas (project pack) (1989, Scholastic)
Butterflies
'Butterfly chart' – Butterfly Farm (Christchurch)
'The life cycle of a silkworm' (chart, cocoon and silk samples) – Silk Education Service
Gossamer frosted paper (good for wings) – Philip and Tacey
Instant themes
Myself
'The milk story' (poster) and *Ourselves* (free pack) – Milk Marketing Board
Starting History: Children (project pack) (1992, Scholastic)

Years 1 and 2
Autumn festivals
Tomorrow's Harvest (free booklet) and *Harvest Ideas for 1992* (free leaflet) – Christian Aid
'Jewish, Hindu and Christian festivals' (charts) – PCET
22 Indian festival stencils – Philip and Tacey
Birds
Getting to Know Birds (video) and 'Barn owl', 'Osprey' and 'Kingfisher' posters and *Early Birds* (activity pack) – RSPB
Birthdays
Lenny's First Journey (video showing the journey of a birthday card) and *Lenny Goes a Long Way* (accompanying story book) – The Post Office Film and Video Library
Starting History: Children (project pack) (1992, Scholastic)
Homes
'Places of worship' (4 charts – Christianity, Islam, Judaism and Sikhism) – PCET
Hindu pack: Hindu temple – CEM
'About the house' (poster) – RoSPA

Minibeasts
'Keeping Minibeasts' (4 charts) — PCET
The NEW Minibeast Mix 'n 'Match (pack) — UNL
Really Useful Insects (pack) — WATCH
Gossamer frosted paper (good for wings) — Philip and Tacey

Myself
'My neighbour's religion' (charts) — PCET
Ourselves (free pack) — Milk Marketing Board
Starting History: Children (project pack) (1992, Scholastic)

Patterns
'Patterns in nature' (photo pack) — PCET

Roads
'What is traffic?' (posters) and 'Top Infant Traffic Information' (workcards) — RoSPA
Roadways (1937) (video of transport history 1918–37) — The Post Office Film and Video Library

Trees
'Beech tree' (poster) in *Child Education* July 1989 (Scholastic)
'Trees of Britain' and 'Woodland Calendar' (posters) — The Tree Council
'Forestry' 1' (poster) — Scout Association
'Task force trees' (free double-sided wallchart) — Countryside Commission
Free children's activity pack — The Woodland Trust

Instant themes
Weather
Weather, Sound and Light (project pack) — Scholastic

School
Play Wise (poster game) and 'Keep Safe' (poster) RoSPA
Starting History: Children (project pack) (1992, Scholastic)

Toys
'In the park' (poster — children playing with Victorian outdoor toys) — Medici
Starting History: Children (project pack) (1992, Scholastic)

Years 3 and 4

Space
'Astronomy: 1' and 'Astronomy: 3' (charts) — Scout Association
The *Solar System* (charts) — PCET
'Make-a-postcard' (rubber stamp) — Philip and Tacey

Secrets
From me 2 u (communication pack) — Crosslinks

Lights
'It's brilliant' (poster) — RoSPA
'Astronomy: 1' and 'Astronomy: 3' (charts) — Scout Association

'Jewish, Hindu, and Christian festivals' (charts) — PCET
'Electricity through the ages' (poster) — Understanding Electricity
Lighthouse Information Pack, free by sending 11" by 1'11" SAE to The Information Officer at the Lighthouse Service
Kodak pinhole camera offer (free by sending a postcard to Eros Mailing Co. Limited)
Electric Lamps — Past and Present (free booklet) — Thorn Lighting

Holidays
Maypole and Country Dancing (cassette and instruction leaflet) and 'Make-a-postcard' (rubber stamp) — Philip and Tacey
Songs from Around the World (cassette) — Unicef-UK

Friends
'Environmental posters' — Friends of the Earth
'Conservation: 2' (chart) — Scout Association

Eggs
'The Egg Story' (free wallchart and activity cards), *Exploring Eggs* (video) and *Food For All* (free pack) — British Egg/Chicken Information Service

Dinosaurs
Dinosaur replicas and actual bones — Stuart Baldwin
'Diplodocus', 'Stegosaurus', 'Triceratops' and 'Tyrannosaurus rex' (posters and dinosaur plastic models) — Natural History Museum

Colours
A Flower Arranger's Guide to Colour Theory (including colour wheel) — NAFAS

Instant themes
Patterns
The Magic Mirror of Escher E. Bruno (1986, Tarquin), *The Mathematical Patterns File* A. Wiltshire (photocopiable patterns) (1988, Tarquin), 'Illusion and Confusion' D. Birmingham (posters), 'Escher' (posters) and 'Can you believe your eyes?' (playing cards) Tarquin
'Patterns' (topic pack) *Junior Education* (1986, Scholastic)
'Patterns in nature' — PCET

Years 5 and 6
Weather
Weather, Sound and Light (project pack) — Scholastic
'Exploring the weather' and 'Greenhouse effect' (posters) — WWF-UK
'Meteorology: 1' (cloud formations) and 'Meteorology: 3' (how to read weather charts) (charts) — Scout Association

and *Interpreting Weather Maps* (free leaflets), and *And Now, Here's the Weather* (colour brochure) — The Met Office

Shopping
The Story of Tea (free booklet) and *Rice, Pasta, Soya and Soya Products* and *Beans, Peas and Lentils* (free fact pack booklets) — Batchelor Foods (Brooke Bond Foods Limited)
The Grains are Great Food (free booklet) — Kelloggs
On Ice (free resource pack) — Frozen Food Educational Service (The British Egg Information Service)
'Food Hygiene with Hy-Genie' (free notes, wallchart and colouring posters) and *Food Sense* (video) — CFL Vision
The Banana Story (video) — Banana Group Education Service
The World in a Supermarket Bag (project pack) — Oxfam Educational
Where Does Our Food Come From? (poster and worksheets) — Oxfam
Food (free fact sheet) — Christian Aid

Our bodies
Miniature skeletons — Heron Education Limited
'The human body' (poster pack) — Scholastic
'Heart poster' (children's poster) — British Heart Foundation
Exploring Ourselves (resource pack) — WWF-UK
The Banana Story (video) — Banana Group Education Service

Islands
The Islanders (1939) (video — people on Eriskay, Guernsey and Inner Farne) — The Post Office Film and Video Library

Games
Board Games from Around the World — Oxfam
Hello World, Life Saving and *The Paper Bag Game* (games and booklets) — Christian Aid
The Great Play Times Games Kit — National Playing Fields Association

Easter
The Egg Story (free wallchart and activity cards), *Food For All* (free project pack) and *Exploring eggs* (video) — The British Egg/Chicken Information Service
Easter Festival stamps — Philip and Tacey
'Palm Sunday and Easter' (freize) — NCEC

Christmas customs
Nativity scenes by famous artists (postcards) — Medici
Christmas Under Fire (1941) (video of Christmas in the underground during the Blitz) — The Post Office Film and Video Library

Communication

The Good Life (free booklet) – Christian Aid
The Story of Communications Around the World (1990) (free brochure) and *Telecommunication Networks* (world map and worksheets) and *Telephones* (free poster) – BT
'Signs and symbols' (chart) – PCET
BT 1 How the Telephone Works and *BT 2/53 Call Across the World* (videos) on free loan – Education Distribution Services
Today's Post Office (1987) and *Men of Letters* (1985) (videos) – The Post Office Film and Video Library
From Me 2 u (communication pack) – Crosslinks

Instant themes
Time

Time Through the Ages (information sheets) – UK Time Ltd
Sundials and Timedials G. Jenkins/M. Bear (working models and a mini book) – Tarquin

An Ideal World

Environmental posters – Friends of the Earth
'Conservation: 2' – Scout Association
'Voice of the children: Children's charter 1992' (free poster) – Voice of the children
'Your community forest' (free poster) – The Countryside Commission
Development Without Destruction (board game) – ActionAid
Hope for the Earth (free leaflet) – Christian Aid

Newspapers

The Paper Bag Game – Christian Aid

USEFUL ADDRESSES

ActionAid, Hamlyn House, MacDonald Road, Archway, London N19 5PG
Stuart Baldwin, Fossil Hall, Boards Tye Road, Silver End, Witham, Essex CM8 3QA
Books for Keeps, 8 Brightfield Road, Lee, London SE12 8QF
British Egg/Chicken Information and Banana Group Education Services, Bury House, 126-128 Cromwell Road, London SW7 4ET
British Heart Foundation, Education Administrator, 14 Fitzhardinge Street, London W1H 4DH
BT Education Service, BT Centre, 81 Newgate Street, London EC1A 7AJ
British Wool Marketing Board, Oak Mills, Station Road, Clayton, Bradford BD14 6JD
Brook Bond Foods Limited, Leon House, High Street, Croydon CR9 1JQ
Butterfly Farm (Christchurch), 6 Westwoods, Box Road, Bathford, Bath BA1 7QE

CBWT, The Confederation of British Wool Textiles Limited, Merrydale House, Roydsdale Way, Bradford BD4 6SB
CEM, Royal Buildings, Victoria Street, Derby DE1 1GW
CFL Vision, PO Box 35, Wetherby, West Yorkshire LS23 7EX
Christian Aid, 35 Lower Marsh, London SE1 7RT
Countryside Commission, John Dower House, Crescent Place, Cheltenham, Gloucestershire GL50 3RA
CRAFTPACKS, 19 Brook Avenue, Warsash, Southampton, Hampshire SO3 9HP
Crosslinks, The Bat, Falmouth Street, Newmarket, Suffolk CB8 0LE
Education Distribution Services, Unit 2 Drywall Industrial Estate, Castle Road, Murston, Sittingbourne, Kent ME10 3RL
Eros Mailing Company Limited, PO Box 2, Central Way, Feltham, Middlesex TW14 0TG
Friends of the Earth, 56-58 Alma Street, Luton LU1 2PH
Galt Educational, Brookfield Road, Cheadle, Cheshire SK8 2PN
Heron Educational Limited, Carrwood House, Carrwood Road, Chesterfield, Derbyshire S41 9QB
Hope Educational Limited, Orb Mill, Huddersfield Road, Oldham, Lancashire OL4 2ST
Kellogg Company of Great Britain Limited, Kellogg House, Talbot Road, Manchester M16 0PU
Learning Development Aids, Duke Street, Wisbech, Cambridgeshire PE13 2AE
Lighthouse Service, The Information Officer, Corporation of Trinity House, Trinity Square, Tower Hill, London EC3N 4DH
Medici Society (Look for products in your local stationers shops)
Meteorological Office, Education Service, Johnson House, London Road, Bracknell, Berkshire RG12 2SY
Milk Marketing Board, Nutrition and Education Department, Thames Ditton, Surrey KT7 0EL
NAFAS, The National Association of Flower Arrangement Societies of Great Britain, 21 Denbigh Street, London SW1V 2HF
NCEC, National Christian Education Council, Robert Denholm House, Nutfield, Redhill, Surrey RH1 4HW
NES/Arnold, Ludlow Hill Road, West Bridgford, Nottingham NG2 6HD
National Dairy Council, 5-7 John Princes Street, London W1M 0AP
National Playing Fields Association, 25 Ovington Square, London SW3 1LQ
Natural History Museum, Visitor's Resource Department, Cromwell Road, London SW7 5BD

Oxfam, 274 Banbury Road, Oxford OX2 7DZ
Philip and Tacey, North Way, Andover, Hampshire S19 5BN
Philip Harris Limited, Lynn Lane, Shenstone, Lichfield, Staffordshire WS14 0EE
PCET, Pictorial Charts Educational Trust, 27 Kirchan Road, London W13 0UD
The Post Office Film and Video Library, PO Box No 145, Sittingbourne, Kent ME10 1NH
RoSPA, Cannon House, The Priory, Queensway, Birmingham B4 6SB (Also available from the Road Safety Officer at the Engineers Department of your Local County Council)
RSPB, The Lodge, Sandy, Bedfordshire SG19 2DL
Scholastic Publications Limited, Westfield Road, Southam, Leamington Spa, Warwickshire CV33 0JH
The Scout Association, The Resource Centre, Gilwell Park, Chingford, London E4 7QW
Shap Working Party, c/o The National Society's RE Centre, 23 Kensington Square, London W8 5HN
Silk Education Service, Parkett Heyes House, Broken Cross, Macclesfield SK11 8TZ
Tarquin Publications, Stradbroke, Diss, Norfolk IP21 5JP
Taskmaster Limited, Morris Road, Leicester LE2 6BR
Technology Teaching Systems Limited, Unit 4 Holmewood Fields Business Park, Park Road, Holmewood, Chesterfield S42 5UY
Thorn Lighting Limited, Public Affairs Manager, Elstree Way, Borehamwood, Hertfordshire WD6 1HZ
The Tree Council, 35 Belgrave Square, London SW1X 8QN
Understanding Electricity, PO Box 44, Wetherby, West Yorkshire LS23 7EH
Unicef-UK, 55 Lincoln's Inn Fields, London WC2A 3NB
UK Time Limited, Marketing Department, CP House, 97 Uxbridge Road, Ealing, London W5 5TN
UNL, University of North London, 166-220 Holloway Road, London N7 8DB
Viscom Limited (See Shell Film and Video Library)
Voice of the Children, PO Box 759, London SE5 8SA
WATCH, (Royal Society for the Conservation of Nature), The Green, Witham Park, Waterside South, Lincoln LN5 7JR
The Woodland Trust, Autumn Park, Dysart Road, Grantham NG31 6LL
WWF-UK, Worldwide Fund for Nature, UK, Panda House, Weyside Park, Catteshall Lane, Godalming, Surrey GU7 1XR